500AD

George Meredith
and English Comedy

George Meredith
and English Comedy

The Clark Lectures for 1969

V. S. Pritchett

RANDOM HOUSE
New York

TO DOROTHY

Chapter One

Chapter One

A WRITER like myself who is neither scholar nor historian, who is not even, in the exclusive sense, a critic, who is utterly ungraduated and lives by standing at his stall in Grub Street every week, must be very moved by the honour of being asked to give the Clark Lectures. I hope it will be understood that I am far from comparing this college to Mr Sapsea in *Edwin Drood* when I say that, like his Miss Brobity, I did feel a "species of awe" when the task was proposed to me; and in the curious, perhaps extra-marital relation between the writer and a great university, I feel (as she did about him) the excitement of "a life-long homage to mind". It is an extraordinary experience to be called to a great seat of learning; for a professional writer is a man with no seat—or rather the only seat he has is his own anxious one. And as he nips from subject to subject, living by the impromptus of the ego, he is mostly up and down or out and about. He is—he depends on being—short of breath. I am told that the profession I belong to is now disappearing fast, along with the printed word and the pleasure of reading it: all the more therefore do I value the chance of speaking in this College where Literature is not merely evaluated but valued, and of making a stand for pleasure and idiosyncrasy. And I take heart from the fact that the learned Clark who gave his name to these lectures had his lighter side. I discover from Mr E. M. Forster that Clark once took a holiday in Spain and wrote a short book about it. It was called *Gazpacho*. I cling to our common Spanish folly.

To call myself a critic would be going too far. I call myself a writer—sometimes an artist. Mr E. M. Forster told a Harvard audience years ago that the critic thinks before he writes, but the artist writes before he thinks. He is in the position of the sculptor who chips away at the stone in order to find the figure, *his* figure, a true self, inside it. The writer's work is a perpetual business of chipping off, a long process of rejection. Scores of obstructive sentences must be chipped away, until the desired sentence or self is made clear. A story or a novel is the residue of innumerable rejected words.

Anyone who has written a story or novel is painfully aware of this. If *what* he has to say has been given to him by God, Nature, Society or Literature itself, the *how* of saying it will be his daily preoccupation. The novelist's "how" has always been important to me as I munch my way from novel to novel. For some writers the question of "how" is simple: they follow the decent conventions. For others, there is either experiment or —much commoner—the struggle to find ways round the natural defects of their talented minds.

It is because we learn so much from the writers who have either got into difficulties or who have a certain vanity in creating them, that I have chosen Meredith as my subject. He is pretty well as vain of his messes as he is of his accepted achievements. He consciously created many obstacles for himself: to take one example, the Idea—and everything was Idea to him—that there was such a thing as absolute Comedy. He had theories about Comedy. He was not thinking of comic relief, humorous observation, farce or satirical orgy. He allowed Laughter as a healthy exercise but Comedy was a rather chaste Platonic Idea. Now the comic tradition in the English novel is a powerful one; it is an alternative to the Puritan tradition; it inspects as it alleviates or makes finer the demands of moral seriousness. Meredith who was a great adapter from the past can tell us a good deal about our comic tradition. What he was trying to do was to conceptualise—which is not a common English habit; and he was conceptualising a dominant tradition of the English novel. In comic irony our novelists have been pre-eminent. It is their most militant and most graceful gift. It has moderated or refined their didactic habit and drawn them closer to nature.

There is a serious initial difficulty in dealing with Meredith now. At any time during the last forty years it has been pretty safe to put on superior and evasive airs and to say that "no one reads him". Just as "no one" reads Scott or Thackeray. We can easily add to the list of such complacencies and they change from generation to generation. But there is no doubt that Meredith not only is but always *was* a difficult case. His small number of distinguished admirers were intense in their delight in him; but his many detractors ended with exasperation. About his very late novel *One of Our Conquerors* which appeared serially in 1890 and 1891, I find this quotation from the critic of *The Athenaeum:*

> it is becoming a common experience to meet cultivated persons who gravely assure us that Meredith is our greatest

living novelist. . . . To us this vogue is inexplicable. . . .
So far from being a great novelist, he does not seem to us
to possess the qualifications which go to the making of a
capable novelist of even the second rank, and, even if those
qualifications were his, their effect would be ruined by a
literary manner which even in these days of affectation and
strain is of unique perversity.

Gissing was among those of the new generation who
held exactly the opposite opinion and so was Oscar
Wilde in his essay on *The Soul of Man Under Socialism*.
So was Robert Louis Stevenson. There is the old joke
that Meredith is a prose Browning and so is Browning.
(The first part of that jeer is really an exact compli-
ment.) Elsewhere, and especially in this university,
Mr E. M. Forster's dig about "The home counties
posing as the universe" has been taken out of context
and thought decisive, as phrases thrown off often are.
But we notice that Mr Forster followed it with the
words:

> And yet he is in one way a great novelist. He is the finest
> contriver that English fiction has ever produced and any
> lecturer on plot must do homage to him.

There *is* a continual "And yet . . ." in both the abuse
and the praise. Henry James called Meredith a sentimental rhetorician "whose natural indolence or con-
genital insufficiency, or both, made him in life, as in
art, shirk every climax, dodge round it, and veil its
absence in a fog of eloquence." James certainly did not
see Meredith as the great contriver. But later he said
"Meredith did the best things best"—a remark that
seems to be double-edged, for one is a bit suspicious of
the phrase "the best things". One is haunted by a

doubt: did the late James make a difference between the "best things" and the glossiest things?

There is something very Meredithian in the comedy of the embarrassed relations of these two old Pretenders —Meredith and the later James, the two most stylistically, obscurely granulated novelists of their period, both so disguised by their love of feint and contrivance that they stumble upon each other like rival magicians in an absurd duel of spells and counter-spells so ineffectual that they can only drive the combatants to exhausted rudeness:

> "Poor old Meredith," James is reported to have said. "He writes these mysterious nonsenses and heaven knows what they all mean."

To which Meredith replies:

> "Poor old James. He sets down on paper these mysterious rumblings of his bowels—but who can be expected to understand them?"

Faced by his critics Meredith has the great disadvantage of being a wit. It makes one an occasion of wit in others and generally of the mortal kind. The joke about the home counties posing as the universe, is mild beside Henley's attempt at sympathy:

> Meredith writes with the pen of a great artist in one hand and the razor of a spiritual suicide in the other.

By acrimonies of this kind, which usually draw blood among literary persons, Meredith seems to have been not greatly affected. He did not blow his brains out, stop writing or reform. He had a splendid vanity. He appears to have been able to shut himself off. He seems not to have been too depressed. He knew his own originality. His lazy, restless mind was always on

13

the move to more epigrams, he was papered all over by egoism and as impervious as Sir Willoughby Patterne. Perhaps for all his lyrical talk of earthiness, he had no blood but simply what he called brain stuff. And in private life, condemned at last to total deafness and locomotor ataxia, he went on living to a great age, giving his perpetual exhibition as a non-stop talker, a pre-manifestation of Shaw's Methuselah, listening to nobody and as if designed by God *not* to listen.

If we look again at Meredith and study his relation to our comic tradition, the task is made easy by Meredith himself. He was a deeply literary novelist: his admiration for the work of his father-in-law, Peacock, shows that. In literature he was a hero-worshipper. As a novelist he was something of a compendium, something of a jackdaw too, with an eye for the bright things. One often has the impression that he writes novels as a critic would write them; that as his pen goes to the paper a critical and a creative artist have a paralysing admiration for each other.

What was in this compendium? Meredith says very little about this and I shall suggest a reason a little later. But I think we may be allowed *our* view of it. It seems to me that our comic tradition is fed by three main streams upon which Meredith drew. I think of them as the masculine, the feminine and the mythic or fantastic. The division is, of course, arbitrary. Sooner or later they will mingle, separate, mingle again. The masculine tradition, if you take this view, runs from Fielding, Scott, Jane Austen, Trollope, George Eliot and on to Kipling, Wells, Waugh, Ivy Compton-Burnett and Anthony Powell. A larger number of brilliant minor figures belong to it. It is sanguine, sociable, positive, morally tough, believes in good sense, even in angered good sense and suspects sensibility. These novelists have paid their dues to society or a moral order. They are on the whole generous, though they have their acerbities. They are robust and hard-headed. They know that, in the long run, feeling must submit to intelligence. Masters like Jane Austen and Fielding also command a variety of comic styles. The undertone can be detected in Jane Austen, in the firm correction of Emma's character, or at the end of *Sense and Sensibility*, in which she is commenting on the complacency of a newly-married couple:

> One of the happiest couples in the world. They had in fact nothing to wish for, but the marriage of Colonel Brandon and Marianne—and rather better pasturage for the cows.

Compare this with the comment of a contemporary novelist, Anthony Powell, another aphorist:

> He also lacked that subjective, ruthless love of presiding over other peoples' difficulties which often makes basically heartless people adept at offering effective consolation.

Or again, sententiousness being natural to this kind of comedy:

> Love had received one of those shattering jolts to which it is peculiarly vulnerable from extraneous circumstances.

Exercise—think of those long walks in Jane Austen's novels—and animal spirits, horseplay, good health have their parts especially in the *male* comic writing of the masculine school. And Fielding established it at that period of bluff settlement and confidence in the early eighteenth century. With him a conventional copy-book morality, dignified by epigram, had come in; later it would be made more subtle; it would appease if it did not satisfy. Those harsh, abstract, political seventeenth-century words like God, King or the State have been replaced by something called "the World" and a very towny World it is. It is inhabited by "men of the world" and "women of discretion". A certain dullness or triteness is relieved by the wild belief in Fortune, in extravagance of character and occasional glimpses of the madhouse. What does "a man of the world" think? He does not think much, or rather he thinks as others do. He is intelligent, but not intellectual. He is a pragmatist. He respects something called "the Way". You follow "the Way of the World" even when you try to reform or civilise "the Way". The title of Congreve's play points to the ruling preoccupation. And what do you *do*? You have adventures, you meet all classes of people, you conduct intrigues. It is a life of action and you have an active but not deeply disturbed moral life. You will be observant of character in its *sociable* relationships. You will rarely see a man or woman alone in their privacy. You will be conscious of being an actor on the social scene and you will be given a certain consequential style, a public manner; its object, aided by the new cult of conversation, is to avoid any sight of the void or horror outside that cannot be governed. Hogarth thinks you can get people off gin by putting them on to beer; only Swift, the half-colonial exile coming from savage Ireland, has a sense of the unsociable horror, only *he* conceives madness and misanthropy. Ireland had no rising middle class.

But suppose you reject the Way, the belief in habit

and behaviour. Suppose you rely on your own mind and not on society's. Suppose you value your privacy, value imagination and sensibility more than common sense. Suppose you live not by clock time, but by the uncertain hours of your feeling. Suppose you live by your imagination or your fantasies. Suppose, with Gray, you think that all you have is your own "pleasing anxious being" and are, perhaps, liable to fright, illness, egocentricity and sin. Then you will be with Sterne in the disorderly, talkative, fantasticating tradition. I call it the feminine, the affectable. It is wayward. Sterne dissolved the sense of order: he saw that we cannot do as we please but that we have a mind that does exactly as it pleases, moves back and forth in time. The "I" is not a fixture; it dissolves every minute; its movements are as uncertain as the transparent jelly-fish as it washes back and forth in the current. Not action, but inaction, being washed along by the tide is the principle, astonished that we are a form of life. The Sterne or feminine strain in our comedy is discernible in Peacock, Dickens, bits of Thackeray, a lot of Meredith again, Lear, Carroll, Saki, Firbank, Virginia Woolf; in Joyce, of course, and in Beckett, in all the experiments and slackeners of social forms. I have seen Sterne described by a young critic, Alvarez, as "cool" and "poised" even existentialist and he is certainly, after being under a cloud, a reviving figure now. For Sterne follows consciousness from sentence to sentence, image to image, wilfully, even in exhibitionist manner. He is receptive to sensation and believes in the mingling of meanings and in the oblique. His feminine strain is not consequential; if he is sententious this is only for the purpose

17

of self-mockery; he may beat a sentimental bosom but his eye is always wandering, leading away his mind. He is a talker and very much a soliloquist. The characters in his novels do occasionally talk to each other, but they are always thinking of something else. They are self-obsessed. They live a good deal in the imagination. The speech they are interested in is the broken syntax of speech-in-the-mind and while that rambles on—not pointlessly, for Sterne is constructing a mosaic—Society, the great gregarious English burden with its call to presentable moral duty, melts away. It is replaced by an immense detail, seen as it might be under a magnifying glass that enlarges and makes everything seem to stand still. This is precisely the effect of trauma or fantasy upon us, for the magnifying glass has shown us at once a real object which is made dream-like by enlargement. Uncle Toby's fuss about the fortifications of Namur is the real fuss of a vegetative old soldier consumed by his memories; but by enlargement it is made to seem a symbol of an extreme modesty. It is to be noted that both Fielding and Sterne tell us when to laugh; but whereas Fielding in his authoritative way, stands back from his novel when he points the finger, Sterne directs from inside it. In fact, he intends that we shall laugh at him when we laugh at his characters. Both novelists digress in order to convey their opinions or the sensible drift of their work; but Fielding's digressions are mainly in his essayish pages, whereas, when Sterne digresses, the whole thing digresses with him. He is writing his novel backwards and very slowly backwards, the surprise lying in discovering what has already happened.

I have called the third strain in our comic tradition mythic or fantastic and this is so adjacent to Sterne's habit that I hesitate over the distinction. But it has to be made because the comedy of Dickens stands a great deal on its own because his genius belongs to a century of violent revolution. We shall find a good deal of Fielding and Sterne in Meredith and well-used. There is a little of Dickens, too, and it is nearly always poor copying and secondhand: the misunderstanding of the comic Dickens has already begun. In the last twenty years or so great stress has been put on the serious socially conscious Dickens, the poetic symbolist, the often melodramatic and violent enemy of social injustice; and the effect of this stress has been to make us treat his comedy as comic relief. (The comic writer never quite overcomes the classical reproof that comedy is an inferior form of writing.) I do not believe that Dickens can be split in two in this way: one part reformer, the other part original English humorist. He represents, for me, his century's powerful release of an important psychological force.

In Dickens's novels we are faced by a vast Gothic structure, a mixture of sprawling Parliament and sinister, often blood-and-thunder theatre. After the pragmatism of the eighteenth century, we have a myth-maker. No one believes in the Way of the World any longer. The Town has gone; it is replaced by the City and the swarm. The Town was a gambler and believed in Fortune. Money was not earned, it was won: an example, useful to comedy, was the abduction of heiresses. Debt was a luxury to be aimed at by the Town. In the City-dominated century, where money has to be

earned, debt is an agony, a shame, a haunting night-
mare that corrodes the next day. The first thing to say
about the comedy of Dickens is that London, the city
itself, becomes the chief character. Its fogs, its smoke,
its noise, its courts, officers, bricks, slums and docks,
its gentilities and its crimes, have a quasi-human body.
London is seen as the sum of the fantasies and dreams
of its inhabitants. It is a city of speeches and voices. The
comedy will be in the fusion of the city's dream life and
its realities. So will the committal to moral indignation.
What we precisely find in this comedy is people's pro-
jection of their self-esteem, the attempt to disentangle
the self from the ineluctable London situation; they
take on the dramatic role of solitary pronouncers. All
Dickens's characters, comic or not, issue personal pronouncements that magnify their inner life. Some are
crude like Podsnap, others are subtle like Pecksniff or
poetic like Micawber, unbelievable like Skimpole,
aristocratic casuists like the father of the Marshalsea,
glossy like the Veneerings. All are actors; quip or
rhetoric is second nature to them. They are strange,
even mad, because they speak as if they were the only
persons in the world. They live by some private idea or
fiction. Mrs Gamp lives by the fiction of the approval of
her imaginary friend Mrs Harris. She, like the other
important comic characters, is a self-made myth. Our
comedy, Dickens seems to say, is not in our relations
with others but in our relation with ourselves, our lives,
our poetry, our genius; it is even our justification in
what Mrs Gamp calls "this wale", this vale of tears. A
character like Pecksniff, may be inferior, as an analysis
of hypocrisy, to Tartuffe or Iudushka in Shchedrin's

The Golovlyov Family, but Dickens does perceive the ghastly fact that the hypocrite is a man who lives by words, destroys other people by words and himself by words that have lost all meaning; yet he is living in his imagination and by pronouncements. Pecksniff says, for example:

> My feelings, Mrs Todgers, will not consent to be entirely smothered like the young children in the Tower. They are grown up and the more I press the bolster on them, the more they look round the corner of it.

The more closely one looks at that grotesque pronouncement, the more accurate it seems about the irrepressible nature of adult feeling. And yet, in those words he has drawn on his sense of himself as a walking history or legend.

This passage is one of the high moments of Dickens's comic art. But we must remember that, like Chekhov, he began his comic writing on the lowest rung of the ladder—the level of the humorist's brainwave and the odd "character" made odder by caricature. But Dickens moved quickly away from the slapstick and arrived at his perception that the histrionic and self-made myth-makers are not simply odd "characters" but are pretty well the norm in the myth city. Imitators of Dickens, in one respect, find that it is the easiest thing in the world, even today, to go out into a London street and pick up people who behave as funny "characters" and as that they record them. But Dickens did far more than that: he saw that they were people whose inner life was hanging out, so to speak, on their tongues, outside their persons. To have the so-called Dickens character served up cold, without benefit of his own or the London or English sense of myth, is painful. And I am afraid that when we get to Meredith's *Evan Harrington* we shall have to say that he, like other novelists since, was cynically imitating. This is strange because fantasy is a most important part of Meredith's comedy.

There is one more thing to say about our comic tradition in the novel, before I return to Meredith. It has one serious defect: the lack of tragic irony. It is extraordinary when one thinks of the influence of *Don Quixote* on the English novelists how they have all—with gentlemanly or middle-class optimism, natural I suppose to an expansive culture which was dramatising its satisfactions—how they have all avoided the tragic conclusion. (The death of Hawser Trunnion in *Peregrine Pickle* is sometimes pointed to, but it is no more than touching.) The Russians, especially Dostoevsky, have gone deeper in comic writing than we have. One has to go back to Elizabethan drama—I think of the death of Falstaff—to see the comic cycle completed. The Elizabethans had not yet been caught by bourgeois sociability and cheerfulness.

When we look at Meredith's methods as a novelist we shall find that he helped himself very freely to many of the ingredients here—to the extent that some critics have accused him of pastiche. I do not think this is true, for it overlooks the difficulties that Meredith put in his own way and it is by his power to interpose and use difficulties that a novelist creates something new and perhaps important.

Meredith's difficulties, his chosen obstacles, I think, are the following:

First there is Meredith himself. He is a persistently, blatantly, intrusive person. He must be in the centre of the stage. In a famous poem Auden suggested that the novelist is a non-person who becomes other people. Meredith is *all* person. Other people become *him*. As a narrator he is always before our eyes, often signposting. The English novelists—Henry James complained—again and again ruin their tales by such personal intervention. But Meredith's novels *are* the intervention. He far outdoes Thackeray who skilfully played the role of master of ceremonies. Meredith acts *his* people off the stage. One has to look to Carlyle and Browning for anything like Meredith's intrusion; and one must conclude that for this there are more interesting reasons than simple egoism. We shall have to make a guess at them. Are they related, for example, to the peculiar intrusiveness which pervades say the work of D. H. Lawrence?

The second stimulating difficulty for Meredith is that he is a poet. I am not going to discuss Meredith's poetry in these lectures. I find it thin. The intrusive person diminishes into an almost furtively biographical figure in many of the verses. He was capable of rhapsody—rather over-exercised rhapsody to my ear—in *Love in the Valley*, but one can see the bearing of this poem on the summer love scene in *Richard Feverel*. The sonnet sequence in *Modern Love* is another matter. Here he comes out with something that he cannot say outright in any of the novels. He spoke out about "modern love" before any of his contemporaries. A

23

genuine Meredith, dispersed by no trick of evasion, has crystallised. One can complain of the occasional romantic cliché, but (in general) the images are hard and clear, the statement is laconic, the scenes are sharp, the whole is concentrated and compressed. It is a paradox, but Meredith, the interminable talker, was made interminable by his passion for compressing, for crystallising, for the economy of telescoping his ideas, and for the abrupt transition from image to image. He was totally fitted to write another great narrative poem like *The Ring and the Book* and one could argue that the literary conventions of his time, the need to earn his living and an intellectual laziness made him choose a stultifying form when he wrote novels. But, from the critic's point of view, the poet in Meredith made him concentrate on intensity, economy and the image in his prose.

The third difficulty for him is that being a poet he was led on to Romance. Romance would allow the rhapsodic; it would suggest either the epic or the tale. It would enable him to put a distance between himself and industrial or commercial England. A congenial choice for him but far less so for us—for since James, Stevenson and possibly Ford Madox Ford, what Romance has there been beyond Firbank and L. H. Myers? Perhaps it is returning in modern novelists like Durrell and Miss Murdoch. But Meredith went further than Romance towards a genre he calls Poetic Romance and treated as High or Artificial Comedy. His people had to be Great People; and his difficulty was to juggle Great People into a contemporary scene which was neither epic nor great. For us the difficulty is to believe in the extraordinary aristocracy he created; the question was and is, could he bounce us into suspending our unbelief? And whether we can regard his scene as anything but Ruritanian? The hopeful answer was that Meredith was a writer of enormous ingenuity and that it would all be a question of making his disparate indeed conflicting gifts come to a single coherent point. Would his feeling be strong enough; would his moral sense be deep enough to bind all together? He could be brilliant but would brilliance be enough?

The binding element was to be what he called the Comic Spirit. What did he have to say about it in his two well-known lectures? They were given in 1877. When he re-read them later on in his life he found— as so many lecturers do, I'm afraid—that lectures need revising and filling out. The lectures were, naturally, a dazzling performance by a considerable actor and mellifluous talker and wit, but one is never quite sure (outside of one or two eloquent passages), what he is saying half the time. He is clearly a romantic idealist. Comedy must be pure comedy, and outside of the ancients, outside of Molière and Congreve, he sees little that is pure. He has a low opinion of the Restoration drama, partly because of its realism, its hoydens and its knockabout morals. He is too much a Victorian to take Charles Lamb's point of defence. He found the people low. The interesting thing is that Meredith concentrates on the theatre, and although he has some general praise for the English novelists, he has little to say in detail. There is not even a quotation. This casual treatment of the novelists is important to our understanding of Meredith's comedy: it is, at heart, conceived of as theatre. His novels will not only be poetic romantic comedies, they will be staged. Comedy, for him, required an aura of court life. The comic poet is rare, he said:

> the semi-barbarism of merely giddy communities and feverish emotional periods, repel him; and also a state of marked social inequality of the sexes.

Comedy appeals to the head rather than to the heart; it is the enemy of the sentimental—that, for him, means the earnest, bemusing, over-bosomed feelings that cheat the Life Force and distract us from our sensual well-being. Comedy is "the fountain of sound sense". Sound sense is a good deal pagan. The English have gone in too much for satire. He objects:

> the laughter of satire is a blow in the back or the face. The laughter of comedy is impersonal and of unrivalled politeness, often no more than a smile . . . the test of true Comedy is that it shall awaken thoughtful laughter.

The idealism is evident, as I have already said, in a sort of Platonic view:

> The Comic, which is the perceptive, is the governing spirit, awakening and giving aim to the powers of laughter, but it is not to be confounded with them; it enfolds a thinner form of them, differing from satire, in not sharply driving into the quivering sensibilities, and from humour in not comforting them and tucking them up.

And he reaches his climax in a rhetorical passage that contains a famous crowd of Meredith's images. Comedy—he says—

has the sage's brows and the sunny malice of a faun lurks at the corners of the half-closed lips drawn in an idle wariness of half tension. That slim feasting smile, shaped like the long bow, was once a big round satyr's laugh, that flung up the brows like a fortress lifted by gunpowder. The laugh will come again, but it will be of the order of the smile, finely tempered, showing sunlight of the mind, mental richness rather than noisy enormity: Men's future upon earth does not attract it; their honesty and shapeliness in the present does, and whenever they wax out of proportion, overblown, affected, pretentious, bombastical, hypocritical, pedantic, fantastically delicate; whenever it sees them self-deceived or hood-winked, given to run riot in idolatries, drifting into vanities, congregating in absurdities, planing short-sightedly, plotting dementedly; whenever they are at variance with their profession and violate the unwritten but perceptible laws binding them in consideration one to another; whenever they offend sound reason, fair justice; are false in humility or mined with conceit, individually or in the bulk—the Spirit overhead will look humanely malign and cast an oblique light on them, followed by volleys of silvery laughter. That is the Comic Spirit.

A fine if frozen piece of eloquence. One would be very glad to rise to those heights in a lecture. Meredith is, as I have said, giving us theatre. But there is an earlier point which is more precise and more suggestive. I refer to his belief that comedy cannot exist without equality of the sexes. There must be cultivated women who can give as good as they get. Meredith is a feminist and often drew women well—in a different way, almost as well as Gissing drew women. But for Meredith, the equality of the sexes meant the contest of the sexes: the sex-battle in Molière's *Le Misanthrope* or in *The Way of the World*, is fundamental to these two comedies. We can see now where his interest lies: it is in the conflict, in the militancy. We shall find these quicken all his novels and that the campaign is (for him) basic and the sign of vitality—the human species shows its vitality by a war-like sorting out, with its brains, of the fittest to survive.

So, if we do not get very much that is definite in Meredith's two lectures, we can see that Meredith understands one important thing about comedy, and its great defence, even today, when everything in the present state of the world seems to shame the possessor of the comic temper. Our perfect novelist of comedy, Jane Austen, is often presented as an example of the felicity of living in a small, cosy world, with one's mind firmly withdrawn from the horror outside. This has always seemed to me untrue. I think of her as a war-novelist, formed very much by the Napoleonic wars, knowing directly of prize money, the shortage of men, the economic crisis and change in the value of capital. I have even seen a resemblance of that second visit to Darcy's house as a naval battle; for notice there how the positions of the people in the drawing room are made certain, where Elizabeth like a frigate has to run between the lines. Militancy and vigilance are the essence of comedy; it brings the enemies within, into the open: pride meets prejudice, sense meets sensibility, the interchange is sharp. The end is clarification and—as Northrop Frye has said—it enacts the myth or illusion of a perennial rebirth. A continually necessary rebirth, for as someone has said, if the curtain were to go up after a comedy we should see a tragedy. And this was indeed true for Meredith. The lecturer on

The Comic Spirit was the poet of *Modern Love*. The question we shall have to ask is whether this sparkling generaliser could separate his crowding ideas, put order on his literary influences, and make them work for him.

Chapter Two

thought of as a product of this shame. Now, it is possible that the very young Meredith was a romantic snob; it is natural to be snobbish when one is young; but he publicly proclaimed the low comedy of his origins in his early, closely autobiographical novel, *Evan Harrington.* He did not even bother to change the names of some of his relatives. When we come to his first important novel, *The Ordeal of Richard Feverel,* another autobiographical element is explicit. There is a close connection, in the plot, between Meredith's life as a son and his life as the father of a son—a father, moreover, deserted by his wife as Meredith himself was deserted. An egoist, he was unforgiving, and in a later novel (*The Egoist*) the psychological meaning of this very personal imbroglio is examined. It is solipsistic:

> Consider him indulgently: the Egoist is the Son of Himself. He is likewise the Father. And the son loves the father, the father the son. . . . Absorbed in their great example of devotion, they do not think of you. They are beautiful.

This is a central theme of his work.

Meredith is very much a tailor-novelist with a large wardrobe who is always trying on new jackets in front of the reader and the new jacket is for himself (and for his characters) a new persona. Carlyle's *Sartor Resartus* was exactly the book for him and one is not surprised by its fertilising influence. In what ideas, in what psychological states—he asks—in what dreams, in what disguises, do we dress up at different stages of our lives? What illusions and what dandified self-satisfactions destroy us? What is our reality? Disguise is one of the fundamental resources of comedy and these disguises (as one sees in Joyce's *Ulysses*) are larks of consciousness. Our fantasies disguise us. Underlying this—there is in Meredith an evident hankering after strenuous nakedness which he seems to yearn for and yet does his late-Victorian best to avoid, falling back on a self-bewildering sleight of hand as at the last moment of striptease he quickly slips a soul over the nearly naked pagan body. For him the dressing up is the thing. It is what interests him, when he looks at the moral condition of society, as it did Carlyle and for some of the same reasons.

This leads to another biographical point. Meredith liked to think of himself as a foreigner in England; if he was the son of a tailor and a bankrupt one at that, he could claim the distinction of foreignness. This was partly because of his Welsh name and the family gossip that the Merediths were really the descendants of nothing less than Welsh princes. So, if Meredith was a snob, he was the most innocent of snobs: the imaginative snob. He had a natural leaning towards the Celtic feeling for giants. (There is nothing odd about this. I remember in Wales once meeting a homely middle-aged lady who was introduced to me as "one of the giantesses of secondary education in Montgomeryshire".) Meredith was very much a professional Celt. To this feeling he added the congenial idea of German gigantism and grotesque. He had been sent to school with the Moravian fathers in Germany and there, instead of being trained in the team spirit, the restraints and conventions of the English public school, he lived by the simple, nature-loving, half-pagan, half-idealistic freedom of this gentle schooling.

Meredith's energetic delight in nature as a power and as a rapturous topography of mountain, wood and stream is very close to German feeling.

The effect of a foreign experience like Meredith's is to stimulate the romantic idea; one becomes the more English and the more foreign for it, for distance gives enchantment to both views; but it also gives one a disturbed and penetrating view of one's own country. Dickens saw an England going mad about heaped-up gold. Meredith is the only English novelist of the nineteenth century to see that rich England was over-fed and gluttonous to the point of stupor. (It is a comic reflection that Meredith was a gourmet, who was eaten up by dyspepsia and driven for a time to live on vegetable juices, an illness he shared with his master, Carlyle. It may be that there is a connection between high-fed language and a disordered stomach.) The England Meredith saw was unlike the England of all our Victorian novelists, except two, and their minds had the foreign touch also: Disraeli the Jew and Gissing, a sort of Orwell who had been down and out in Manchester and Chicago. Disraeli saw English politics operatically; Gissing, with something like the eye of an outcast emigrant.

One can argue that there was nothing very exceptional about Meredith's foreign nostalgias in Victorian England. The Court was germanified; Carlyle and George Eliot were deep in German literature; the passion for Italy absorbed Ruskin and the Brownings, produced Clough's superb *Amours de Voyage*, and engrossed English politicians. Gladstone entered his feelings of love, in his early Diaries, in Italian. The

36

English imagination had moved away from the voyages of discovery, and on to the spectacle of Europe. Also, obsessed by colonising, the Victorians colonised history, bringing the Gothic and the medieval into the mind, either feeling that their conquest of *machine* power had given them the *romantic* power to bring Venice to the English pub and villa—as Ruskin complained—and to cover the ugliness of the new dispensation with the clothes of the past. A railway station becomes a cathedral, an insurance office a cloister. Victorian London itself looks like an attempt, by an exuberant looting of history, to distract the city from what its life is really like and what it is doing. A romantic character like Meredith's Richmond Roy, a pseudo royalty, is at one with a city that is pretending to live in another age; and Meredith's own romanticism is at one with the national or, at any rate, the middle class determination to live in an imaginary world and a real one at the same time.

But what sets Meredith apart is the effect of his education in Germany. Several of his novels are really *educations sentimentales*. Foreign education must have freed him (just because he *was* abroad) from defensiveness or aggressiveness about his inferior social position; he could assume any role he wished and if he was caught in the English class system, he could elect himself to membership of a private aristocracy. He could be whatever he liked without falling into the English habit of turning a class worry into a moral worry. It may, of course, be a loss when we lose a stimulating national obsession—there is a lot to be said for having the evils of one's age—but the loss frees one for independent observation. The price Meredith paid for the ease of his emancipation from religious doubt and social pessimism was, that he became far too back-slapping in his hearty paganism and in his easy and too personal flirtation with Darwinism and the idea of the survival of the fittest. He feels his characters must be, in some way, superb. But the positive influence of foreign education upon Meredith as a novelist was to make him look at character in a new way. When D. H. Lawrence (also a self-made foreigner in English life) attacked the traditional attitude to character in the English novel. he was enlarging a ground Meredith had already opened; there is a good deal of Meredith in Lawrence whether that influence was conscious or was simply in the air at the time. It is found in Lawrence's lyricism, but above all in the sardonic and reiterated stress on a single essence in his characters.

Now Meredith has few "characters" in the traditional sense, except in *Evan Harrington* and in one or two other places where he was imitating Dickens. (One original is Skepsey, the clerk and servant and fanatical boxer in *One of Our Conquerors*.) Both Meredith's belief in what he called Idea in comedy, and the fact that he was before everything a poet, made him see people as poetic or intellectual statements. They are essences or forces. Richard Feverel is Youth. Patterne is the Egoist. Victor Radnor is Power. But they are not allegorical; they are not humours. They have a living vehemence. They are psychological patterns. They are saturated in Meredith; their engine is his. They are driven along by him, by his beliefs, his mannerisms, his epigrams, his views about sentimentality, nature, blood and soul. They are individualities before they are persons. They are a species grafted on to him. They cannot escape him, just as—after the mining stories and *Sons and Lovers*—no one escapes Lawrence. They haven't a chance in *The Prussian Officer*, in *St Mawr* or *The Fox*. Of course Lawrence's intrusive person is more forceful and vital, more *inside*, than Meredith's. Meredith saw people from the outside; but Lawrence's incantations are as intrusive as Meredith's oratorical parades before the reader.

To the extent that he was freed of traditional character Meredith replaced it by another interest— psychological enquiry. He half-regretted this. He understood that he was sensitive to what he called "the morbidities". He wrote to a publisher:

> Much of my strength lies in painting morbid emotion and exceptional positions. . . . My love is for epical subjects— not for cobwebs in a putrid corner, though I know the fascination of unravelling them.

The opposed directions of his talent, torn between epic and morbidity, Romance and anti-Romance, the poetic and the ironic, set up a central conflict. The device he used was to push forward his glittering and scepti- cal person. Several critics in the '20s—the astute young Mr Priestley was one—saw in Meredith a link with contemporary novelists, Lawrence and especially Virginia Woolf and E. M. Forster: with the personal voice, the pursuit of the mind's dramas of association, the feeling for image, and the emancipation from Mr Bennett and Mrs Brown. By the '20s the patronising of Meredith had already begun, but the link is there. The personal conversational voice is clearly the mark of Meredith's immediate successors. It is evident in *The Longest Journey* and in *The Waves*. And is implicit in the doctrine of the supreme value of personal relationships and particularly in the Bloomsbury belief in extravagantly rational detachment.

By a paradox E. M. Forster's admirable account of Meredith's mastery of plot and contrivance shows (and perhaps unintentionally) the real link between Meredith and his successors in the next generation; but for the working writer, painfully learning to use tools that are new to him, these links are in technique, in the study of how things are done. Except for the reference to "faking" which is gratuitous, for, alas, all the most important novelists have faked somewhere or other, Mr Forster's remarks on Meredith as a technician are not only excellent in themselves, but describe certain things common to his own generation. Mr Forster says:

> A Meredithian plot is not a temple to the tragic or even to the Comic Muse, but rather resembles a series of kiosks most artfully placed among the wooded slopes which his people reached by their own impetus and from which they emerge with altered aspect. Incident springs out of character and alters that character. People and events are closely connected, and he does it by the means of these contrivances. They are often delightful, sometimes touching, always unexpected.

"Not a temple, but a series of kiosks"—how well that describes the Meredithian scene and how the art of moving from kiosk to kiosk, under personal impetus, caught on in the next generation!

But whether one thinks of Meredith as a Sultan among his kiosks or as a brilliant craftsman working in mosaic, it is obvious that he was unlucky in the commercial demands made upon the novelist in the nineteenth century. The novelist depended economically on serialisation and on the demand for three volumes. All the Victorians padded outrageously, as Gissing said, at the rate of 4,000 words a day. This was no difficulty for the recklessly inventive. You simply sprawled as the new disorderly Victorian cities sprawled. But sprawling is dangerous to the novelist who is first a poet and then a wit. Six hundred pages of poetry and wit, in which every line and image is intense, in which there is an infinitude of small, separate visions, choke the mind and weary the eye.

To read some stretches of Meredith's prose is like living on a continuous diet of lobster and champagne: lobster done in every known sauce and champagne only too knowingly addressed as the Veuve. And yet the difficulties of his style have surely been exaggerated. Goodness knows, the modern reader has been brought up on difficult prose. He has been used to cracking images in his teeth like nuts. The later James and Proust are difficult writers. After Joyce, after the difficult poets, after all the unexplained, cinematic transitions of visual picture in the mind, surely Meredith's style ought to be easy. It is simply a matter of getting used to it. There *is* a difference between Meredith's difficulty and the kind we are used to. He is concerned with the actions of his characters or their description; he wishes to push forward; but cannot resist striking an attitude or going off at a tangent, so that in fact his narrative often stands still. He is like a walker, continually stopping to enthuse instead of getting on. And there are times when excess of brain turns him to vulgarity and when his prose scatters and disconnects what should be, and is intended to be, a harmonious flow.

The prose of his first book of tales, an allegory of his own making and the fruit of his youthful taste for the *Arabian Nights*, was mannered but simple enough; as George Eliot said in her very favourable review, the book was not pastiche, its fantasy was original. The portrait of Shagpat asleep outside his shop is excellent *because* of its fantastic touches:

> He who lolled there was indeed a miracle of hairiness, black with hair as he had been muzzled with it, and his head as it were a berry in a bush by reason of it. Then thought Shibly Bagarag, "'Tis Shagpat! If the mole could swear to him surely can I". So he regarded the clothier, and there was naught seen on earth like the gravity of Shagpat. He was as sleepy as a lion cased in his mane; as an owl drowsy in the daylight.

The only thing that puzzled the critics was the symbolism of the tales.

There is nothing to complain of in the prose of *Richard Feverel*. It has several manners and one can recognise the echoes of Lamb. *Harry Richmond* is straightforward, and Fielding-ish; no colliding of metaphors here. *Diana of the Crossways* has no obstructive manner. Before it *The Egoist* and *Beauchamp's Career* have abrupt stylised passages; the old chef cannot resist—especially in *The Egoist*—doing a *flambé* or tossing a pancake, but one accepts a certain amount of twirling and brandy flash when Meredith is feeling effusive. I have only a limited sympathy with Meredith's critics in his own time, who were conditioned to admire the all-weather, all-purpose prose in which important nineteenth-century novels were written.

As an avowed comedian in terms of poetic romance, Meredith thought of images, whether lyrical or comic, as promoters of dramatic movement. They are meant to give energy. The mind is made to give a leap into fantasy and, with it, the scene is agitated. Meredith's prose was the imagination's revolt against the public prose of the main stream of novelists—the style that derived from what Scott called Big Bow Wow. It stands for the poet's impulse to work from inside. The image is the natural mode of consciousness; the image is meant, again and again, to catch a consciousness, as it passes from one feeling or experience to another. It is either a dramatic device or a form of gaiety or play. Meredith is rarely clumsy when he is, so to say, "imaging out" young love and catching its changes. Landscape and seascape are used to describe aspects of love or other emotions. There is an important moment in the love duel between Willoughby Patterne and Clara Middleton when Clara is suddenly frightened just for a split second that Willoughby is going to give her the moral blackmailer's kiss. The moment is described in these words:

> "You are cold, my love? You shivered."
> "I am not cold," said Clara. "Someone, I suppose, was walking over my grave."
> The gulf of a caress hove in view like an enormous billow hollowing under the curled ridge.
> She stooped to pick a buttercup; the monster swept by.

One must see these images in their context and then they no longer seem too large, outlandish or prolonged. They perfectly evoke and activate a feeling which is passing, brief but momentous. He is recording one of those tremors of association that the sensibility of a poet will infallibly hit upon.

Meredith is indeed a prose Browning and all the better for it. Take these lines from the *Flight of the Duchess:*

> And what was the pitch of his mother's yellowness,
> How she turned as a shark to snap the spare-rib
> Clean off, sailors say, from a pearl-diving Carib,
> When she heard, what she called the flight of the feloness

Compare that with Willoughby Patterne forced to give up Clara in *The Egoist:*

> Laocoon of his own serpents, he struggled to a certain magnificence of attitude in the muscular net of constrictions he flung around himself. Clara must be given up. Oh bright Abominable! She must be given up: but not to one whose touch of her would be darts in the blood of the yielder, snakes in his bed; she must be given up to an extinguisher.

High stuff and not as concrete as Browning, but you *are* made to feel the bodily, physical shape of the feeling. It is in the nerves and muscles. The three obscure writers of the nineteenth century, Carlyle, Browning and Meredith, have the visual wit of those who stuck gargoyles and heraldic beasts on pseudo-medieval buildings, because the century's imaginative life was histrionic and loved the grotesque. The scene has to be itself and yet contain the imagination's energy. And what Browning wrote to Ruskin, in his defence of *his* own style, is pure Meredith:

> You would have me paint it all plain out, which cant be; but by various artifices I try to make shifts with touches

and bits of outline which succeed if they bear the conception from me to you. You ought, I think, to keep pace with the thought, tripping from ledge to ledge of my "glaciers" as you call them, not poking your alpenstock into holes.

But, except in his lyrical passages, Meredith is perhaps a collector of styles rather than an innovator and he was not a success when, under the political influence of Carlyle, he also took over patches of his prose. The following is Carlyle who sees the image as action:

> Let but Teufelsdröckh open his mouth, Heaschrecke's also unpuckered itself into a free doorway, besides his being all eye and ear, so that nothing might be lost and then, at every pause in the harangue, he gurgled out his pursy chuckle of a cough-laugh (for the machinery of laughter took some time to get in motion, and seemed crank or slack), or else his twanging nasal, Bravo! Das glaub'ich.

This is good Carlyle, and good Wyndham Lewis, too, Twentyish stuff. But the effect of too much Carlyle was to make Meredith vulgar. An affecting scene between lover and mistress in *One of Our Conquerors* ends happily but in tears and Meredith comes galumphing in with this comment:

> "We cry to Women: Land Ho! A land of palms after storms at sea, and at once they inundate us with a deluge of eye-water."

And Nataly, the weeping lady, is made to apologise to her lover:

> "I am like . . . the tearful woman whose professional apparatus was her soft heart and a cake of soap."

Instead of saying "to steal a glance", he will call this "the petty larceny of the optics". This is not energising

45

Teuton but facetious English gentility. (On the other hand to describe parsons as "the turncocks of one water company" is good.) Meredith writes in *The Amazing Marriage*—a passage that upset Edmund Gosse [The scene is a gambling table]:

> He compared the creatures dabbling over the board to summer flies on butchers' meat, periodically scared by a cloth. More in the abstract they were snatching at a snapdragon bowl. It struck him that the gamblers had thronged in an invitation to drink the round of seed time and harvest at one gulp. Again they were desperate gleaners, hopping, skipping, bleeding, amid a whizz of scythe blades, for small wisps of booty. Nor was it long before the presidency of an ancient hoary Goat-Satan might be perceived, with skew-eyes, nursing a hoof on a tree.

Four attempts to find a metaphor for gambling when one alone is required: one for the commentator and a clumsy one at that. And they are all—unless in the mind of a farmer—inapt. Meredith has not only intruded personally, but his mind is not made up. It is all hit or miss. If images are meant to activate, too many images brawl. This passage stands still. We can cut out the butcher's meat and the snapdragon bowl at once; they collide with the gleaning. The only good image in the passage is "the skew-eye of the goat". How could Meredith who took great care with his style, pass a paragraph like that?

The bother in those disastrous passages is that the mind is the mind of Meredith the artist showman, and that the final impression is one of great messy orchestral clash, ending in anti-climax. In *One of Our Conquerors*, a late novel in which one would have thought he would have learned his lesson, Meredith sets out on two or three panoramic scenes: the sight of London Bridge at the morning rush; and later, the sight of the crowd moving home westward at the end of the day. Both pieces are a hopeless mixture of the poetic and grotesque because they are not really made to mix. The workers have stopped work:

> No longer mere concurrent atoms of the furnace of business (from coal dust to sparks rushing, as it were, on respiratory blasts of an enormous engine's centripetal energy) their step is leisurely to meet the rosy Dinner which is ever at see-saw with the God of light in his fall.

This sounds like, "Sun down; Dinner up". As for the sunset—and all Victorian writers and painters have a compulsion to describe sunsets—Meredith thinks of it in this way:

> It is a Rape of the Sabines overhead from all quarters, either one of the winds brawnily larcenous; and London, smoking royally to the open skies, builds images of a dusty fray for possession of the portly dames. There is immensity, swinging motion, collision, dusky richness of colouring, to the sight; and to the mind idea.

Now this is not simply bad writing: it is ambitious bad writing. It is an outburst, for the rest of the novel is done in a plainish style. But if one reads this whole chapter called *The London Walk Westward* one sees that Meredith did have a conscious, intelligent intention. He is staging London. He imagines a literary Rajah looking at the London scene with an Oriental eye who has the idea that Londoners march eastward for fuel and westward for food. The scene is a piece of theatre. He is explicit about this.

> According to the Stage directions [he writes] the Rajah and His Minister *Enter a Gin Palace*. It is to witness a

47

service that they have learned to appreciate as Anglicanly religious.

And there we have the key to this clumsy cleverness. Where have we read such things before? Meredith has taken them from the burlesque in Fielding. In Fielding it has dramatic effect. The artifice is clear. A classical mind controls it. In Meredith, German romantic grotesque has muddled it, and the cleverer he is the worse the muddle. The sunset hour may very well be London's sentimental hour, in which fancies are muddled: the stream of consciousness is probably pretty thick with stuff like this at that time of day; but for that reason it calls for a precise or selective describer.

There is no objection to Meredith putting his scenes on the stage. The tradition of Fielding, so strongly influenced by the theatre, is important to English comedy. One kind of comedy depends on seizing an incident or scene, setting it apart or aslant from its context—the fight between the women in the churchyard in *Tom Jones*, the rituals of the debtors in the Marshalsea scenes in *Little Dorrit*. The writer of comedy has to shape and form his scenes. Meredith is simply unsuccessful in staging crowds; he is effective in staging individual people.

The fact is that Meredith, the tailor and disciple of Teufelsdröckh, moves towards fantasy and abstraction the better to make his psychological point. The example of Sir Willoughby Patterne's leg shows him at work. There are two pages of it and it establishes Sir Willoughby's person, his character, and their effect on other people. For Meredith our ambience and what we suggest to the fancies of others is part of ourselves: we exist as histories, as poems in the minds of others:

> The leg of the born cavalier is before you: and obscure it as you will, dress it degenerately, there it is for the ladies who have eyes. You *see* it: or, you see *he* has it. Miss Isabel and Miss Eleanour disputed the incidence of the emphasis, but surely, though a slight difference of meaning may be heard, either will do: many, with a good show of reason, throw the accent on leg. . . . Mrs Mountstuart signified that the leg is to be seen because it is a burning leg. There it is and it will shine through. He has the leg of Rochester, Buckingham, Dorset, Suckling; the leg that smiles, that winks, is obsequious to you, yet perforce of beauty self satisfied; that twinkles to a tender midway between imperiousness and seductiveness, audacity and discretion; between "you shall worship *me*" and "I am *devoted* to you" is your lord and slave alternatively. It is a leg of ebb and flow and high tide ripples.

(In that sentence we see Meredith as usual swapping into the wrong image. But he rescues himself and comes to the decisive point)

> Such a leg, when it has done with pretending to retire, will walk straight into hearts of women. Nothing so fatal to them.

Unmistakably, that leg is a sexual symbol. Meredith intends that. Patterne is as male, apparently, as Darcy was. The leg is not for the drawing room alone. But Meredith quickly retreats from the unmannerly idea.

> A simple seeming word of this import is the triumph of the spiritual and where it passes for coin of value, the society has reached a high refinement: Arcadian by the aesthetic route.

There you have the late-Victorian pretender, rising above his insinuation.

49

There is a surprising passage of self-criticism in *Beauchamp's Career*, in the scene in which Beauchamp is explaining the difference between the Conservative and Liberal parties to Miss Halkett. It goes:

> (Liberalism) stakes too much on the chance of gain. It is uncomfortably seated on half a dozen horses; and it has fed them, too, on varieties of corn.

Miss Halkett replies:

> I know you wouldn't talk down to me but the use of imagery makes me feel that I am addressed as a primitive intelligence.

Beauchamp replies:

> That's the fault of my trying at condensation, as the hieroglyphists put an animal for a paragraph. I am incorrigible you see.

Meredith *is* incorrigible and if he wearies one it is because he is the wit who always wins. Of course Beauchamp is not Meredith, but the important characters in Meredith are always extremists because they have to carry this thing he called Idea. He has another comment in *Diana of the Crossways* about Diana's writing, which reverts to the Arcadian argument I quoted just now. It obviously contains glances at his own prose. Diana had been hurt, therefore she plumped for metaphor. He writes in her defence and his own:

> Metaphors were her refuge. Metaphorically she would allow her mind to distinguish the struggle she was undergoing, sinking under it. The banished of Eden had to put on metaphors, and the common use of them has helped largely to civilise us—the sluggish of intellect detest them, but our civilisation is not much indebted to that major faction.

I have spoken at length about the excesses in Meredith's prose and have said that they show a mind that tends to disperse its gifts and to have difficulty in finding a common ground. But he does find it once he has settled in to his work, either in the well-known lyrical interludes—the river scene and storm scenes in *Richard Feverel*—and in his mastery of ironic narrative and commentary where his psychological curiosity subdues the actor. Then his inventiveness as a poet brings gaiety to a prose which is even more an essayist's than the prose of a novelist. And it is not so far from the agitated prose of those modern writers who seem to have sensed that the prose of the future will be heard and seen, and perhaps never read.

Chapter Three

Chapter Three

WHEN Mr Forster complained that Meredith's cricket was not cricket, the trains were not trains and that the country houses were conjectural, our reply must be: "No, of course, they were not. He was writing Romance." Meredith himself rejected everyday realism; his first book *The Shaving of Shagpat* was a fantasy.

It is difficult to say exactly what a Romance should do or not do. If we except Jane Austen, the English novelists are incurable mixers; they have evidently thought they were entitled to move some things out of focus: it would be a way of making meaning emotional. If Meredith's country houses and cricket matches float in the air, his bye-elections are very real; if his people are inflations their sensibilities and the content of their minds are not. What Henry James said in his preface to *The American* when he re-read it, comes nearest to an account of the mixed practice:

> The only general attribute of projected romance that I can see, the only one that fits all its cases, is the fact of the kind of experience with which it deals—experience, liberated, so to speak; experience disengaged, disemboweled, disencumbered, exempt from the conditions that we usually know how to attach to it and, if we so wish to put the matter, drag upon it.

He goes on:

> The balloon of experience is in fact of course tied to the earth, and under that necessity we swing, thanks to a rope

of remarkable length, in the more or less commodious car of the imagination; but it is by the rope we know where we are, and from the moment the cable is cut we are at large and unrelated: we only swing apart from the globe—though remaining as exhilarated, naturally, as we like, especially when all goes well. The art of the romancer is, "for the fun of it", insidiously to cut the cable, to cut it without our detecting him.

As for being a drug—yes, Romance *is* hallucination:

There are [James goes on] drugs enough, clearly, it is all a question of applying them with tact; in which the way things *don't* happen may be artfully made to pass for the way they do.

The general advantages of Romance for the novelist is that in disposing of a too identifiable society, it frees him for the expressing of psychological insights and for telling stories that embody a fundamental myth or fable. It drains away everyday domestic character and circumstance from the novel and replaces these by the psyche floating free and heightened and magnified so that it is clearer to the poet's and psychologist's eye. And in Meredith's Romance—notably in *Beauchamp's Career*—circumstance and society have a psyche also. Beauchamp's England is an inner, if partial, version of the outer England which was circumstantially described by the realists of "the condition of England" movement. Meredith's analysis of egoism in *The Egoist* is tied to the notion that egoism is the very soul of the rich and ruling classes in the England of the '70s.

But because society had a psyche in Meredith's novels his people do not float in complete freedom and he was aware of the difficulty mentioned by Henry James: to palm off the way things don't happen as the way they do. Meredith's strange style was a device for doing this, for linking his Romance to a real world. He was divided, as I said in Chapter Two, between his longing for the grand epic subject and his skill in writing about what he called the morbid intricacies of human feeling. Here he was often very telling. Under the hearty and effervescing Romantic there was a mordant and self-punishing man. The Romantic is bound to be punished and so in the forefront of Meredith's mind is the firm idea of the *Ordeal*. We are on earth to be tried by fire. We are to be tested for integrity and good sense. The idea appears in his very first novel, *The Shaving of Shagpat*, and it is even present in the exquisite little surface farce of *General Ople and Lady Camper*.

One of the odd but I suppose very Victorian things about Meredith's idea is that the ordeal is not only spiritual—we must suffer until we are purified of Romantic dross—but it is physical. Bodily pain is necessary as well as inevitable; the thing to do is to know how to take a beating or a punch-up, purge oneself by laughter and recognise the value of the discipline. The barber in *Shagpat* is frequently beaten. There is a chapter called "the thwackings"—note how Meredith turns a fact into a general Idea—and after all the physical thwackings of Fate he is free of his conceit, his innocence and illusions; now he can win the Princess. So little is really known about Meredith's inner life; he is complex and became hermetic, despite the flow of talk and letters. But I think a contemporary psychologist (who had no doubts about the possibility of getting personal evidence about an author from his works) would pounce upon the case of General Opie. Plagued to the point of nervous breakdown by the practical jokes of a captivating widow, the General finds her the more irresistible the more punishment increases. We find this very strange even very bold passage, that nowadays raises an eyebrow:

> . . . Many who have journeyed far down the road, turn back to the worship of youth, which they have lost. Some are for the graceful worldliness of wit, of which they share just enough to admire it. Some are captivated by hands that can wield the rod, which in earlier days they escaped to their cost. In the case of General Opie, it was partly her whippings of him, partly her penetration. . . . You hear old gentlemen speak fondly of the switch; and they are not attached to pain, but the instrument revives their feelings of youth. . . . For in the distance, the whip's end may look like a clinging caress instead of a stinging flick.

Later on, in *Beauchamp's Career*, we shall come upon the famous dramatic episode of the beating up of Dr Shrapnel, the old Radical. To the violent Victorians who seem to have taken thrashing as a matter of course, this ugly episode was not shocking. The beating up of Bradlaugh outside the House of Commons was thought of as satisfactory and character-building for Bradlaugh: it destroyed his character. But after the Shrapnel episode, Meredith finds that the two enemies distantly respect each other. It is not a great comfort, for Dr Shrapnel was old and sick and the beating hurries on his death. The point I come to is that Meredith treats this as a subject for comedy: it is true that local society is shocked by the Squire's brutality and that Beauchamp is savage with indignation and is henceforth uncompromising in his Radical career; it is true also that

Meredith's own Radical hate of an overfed and brutal ruling England comes out. All the same his morbid eye cannot resist treating the subject as comedy. The sight of two old men whacking away at each other is grotesque, and he cannot resist it. We cannot be quite sure whether he is harking back to Fielding's love of a little horseplay, sinning by literary association; or whether the pain of early personal experience has given him the taste and the voice that laughs off the effects, in the name of sanity.

But the important ordeal is spiritual. The soul has to pass through fire. And what has to be burned away? Pride above all and self-delusion. The business of comedy is ruthlessly to expose the false emotions and the false image of oneself and the purpose of comedy is to establish sanity. This is the theme that dominates all Meredith's novels; it is his only important theme. His hero should emerge at the end, fitted at last to face life. By nature his heroes are honourable but wilful extremists. They live in the imagination, which gives them a tremendous energy.

The intensity which Meredith brought to his theme is personal and bitter. It is stated in the cynical reflection of Adrian, the so-called Wise Youth and parasite in *The Ordeal of Richard Feverel*, after young Richard has been pulled out of his rick-burning scrape. The passage is well-known—one has to stomach the studied Shakespearean echo in the middle: Coleridge as well, and the reference to the theatre:

> Experience? You know Coleridge's capital simile. Mournful you call it? Well! All Wisdom is mournful. 'Tis therefore, coz, that the Wise do love the Comic Muse. Their

own high food would kill them. You shall find great poets, rare philosophers, night after night on the broad grin before a row of yellow lights and mouthing masks. Why? Because all's dark at home. The Stage is the pastime of great minds.

The important thing for us is that it was in the year of his wife's flight that Meredith wrote his second ordeal story, *The Ordeal of Richard Feverel.* It was published in 1859, the year of Darwin's *Origin of Species* and of *Adam Bede,* George Eliot's first full length novel that was to become the lengthiest bestselling novel since *Waverley.* Meredith hoped for an equal success. He did not get it. He was praised thoroughly by a few and was doing well when the influential critics called the book prurient and Mudie's all powerful library withdrew it. Among the novels that attacked the Victorian father, and in spite of being brokenbacked, it has lasted. *Richard Feverel* is an extremist's book—the extremism is intellectual and poetic—and extremists are apt to exhaust themselves when they get to the critical point of a work of art. They are apt, as Meredith always is, to become perverse and at the very point where they are masters.

Once the rope is cut *The Ordeal of Richard Feverel* floats free as a bold and believable psychological novel. The world of Romance is established first by making the hero and his father enormously rich and handsome; by the invention of Sir Austin Feverel's preposterous yet idealistic System; by exposing it to idyllic pagan love and by establishing Richard as the ideal Youth, dedicated to virginity. This will lead to disaster. For the poetic part Meredith went to Shakespeare in the story of Romeo and Juliet; but the tragedy unfolds in the setting of comic irony. Sir Austin is a monomaniac; he hopes by his educational system to conduct his son, with a father's love, through the stages of growing up, which he calls Simple Boyhood, the Blossoming Season, the Magnetic Age, the period of Probation. He will enter a Manhood worthy of Paradise—in other words he will inherit the father's great estate, conduct it honourably, marry a carefully selected wife of the right social class, and produce the children that guarantee the immortality of a superb social order. The System ends by turning a pleasant boy into a man almost as maniacal and masked as the father. For the flaw is that Sir Austin has become a *scientific* systematiser— Meredith hates science—because he is a misogynist whose pride has been injured by an unfaithful wife. Woman is the serpent—the image of Woman as serpent recurs continually in Meredith's accounts of passion. Sir Austin has written a tiresome book of Aphorisms called *The Pilgrim's Scrip*, and which contains a ferocious statement called *The Great Shadock Dogma*. Women must be utterly opposed:

> To withstand them (that is, Women) must we annihilate our Mothers within us: die half!

And Meredith goes on:

> The poor gentleman, seriously believing Woman to be a Mistake had long been trying to do so. Had he succeeded he would have died his best half, for his mother was strong within. The very acridity of the Aphorisms, the Great Shadock Dogma itself, sprang from wounded softness, not from hardness.

Despising women, he gives all his love to his son and the System is the result of it. And in one sense, the

System appears liberal, if unduly shrewd. Sir Austin has attached to his family a parasitic and worldly young tutor called The Wise Youth who never commits himself, and takes his pleasures on the sly; a hearty manly victim of *mésalliance*, called Austin Wentworth—typical of Meredith to confuse the reader by introducing two Austins—and an uncle Hippias, a foolish, dilapidated and dyspeptic rake, the very sight of whom will be a warning against loose living. There is a grim sister and a sentimental widow (Lady Blandish) who adores the boy and who hopelessly longs to marry Sir Austin. There is material for excellent comedy and Meredith manages it well. Critics have been irked by the device of the much quoted *Pilgrim's Scrip*. To us such devices are silly and knowingly facetious. They are a mannerist's idea and come down from Fielding—Kipling's idea of the Law is also a development of it—the practical function is to supply linking commentary or stage directions; it helps to separate the staged scenes and Meredith's idea is that most scenes should be stylised and staged. But upon this artificial scheme lyricism blows in. It is spring in the Thames Valley, Richard is sexually awakened, falls in love with a farmer's daughter, against all the Rules and eventually gets her to elope with him just at the moment when Sir Austin has gone to look for some eligible debutante. These proper young girls on the marriage market are a sickly lot. (There is great stress on physical health in Meredith; in a period given to the idealisation of sickness, this robustness must have caused uneasiness.) They are out of touch with Nature. And Nature, aided by scenery, is the enemy of the System. When the scandal breaks, Sir Austin refuses to see his son and there is a battle of two prides. The son—who returns his father's love—will not ask his blessing and forgiveness unless he receives his wife as well.

It is at this point, the most extreme, of the drama, that the novel breaks down. Meredith's task was to prolong the battle, for he wishes to show—and as a good psychologist he should show it—that a boy brought up on Sir Austin's system must have been perverted by it; but how is one to do that when the boy and girl are beautifully in love, having passed ecstatically from innocence to fulfilment. He is forced to separate them; and that would be fine if the separation were short. But he prolongs it, days pass into weeks, weeks into inexplicable months. In this Meredith never convinces us, despite his ingenuity. In fact he is clumsily stealing the time to show us that Richard's sexual ecstasy has revived his idealism in a preposterous form. Convinced that his father is wrong about women and that the bad marriage system has ruined the sex, he virtually abandons his young wife! What for? In order to reform London prostitutes and the loose-living, of whose existence he had been ignorant until then. He intends to return like a feminist Galahad to his wife. Of course he is soon tricked into infidelity with a woman he believes he is rescuing—it is brilliantly perceptive and good fantasy that the woman dresses up as a man in this theatrical episode—and goes off in horror to the Continent. The news that his wife has had a child at last brings him back, but he goes off to fight a duel with his trickster in France. He is wounded and his young wife goes mad. The effect of

Sir Austin and his System has been to kill the boy's heart.

The weakness for complicating his narrative in the way I have noted, once the dénouement is reached, is chronic in Meredith's novels and no doubt part of his morbidity. Perhaps he realised he was a static novelist of set scenes and thought he was adding the action and suspense that were expected by the reader of the padded-out three volume novel. But he was really a contriver I think because he lacked calm and large powers of invention. He was certainly indulging the love of his own cleverness. Yet even when he is going to pieces Meredith can write a fine scene that will restore the shape and symbolism of the tale. The lyrical writing of the early love scenes is matched by the famous storm scene at the end, and allowing for a certain storm rhetoric, it does contain fine lines. Going back over the story, one sees how closely Meredith moves with the moving mind of his hero. How discreetly he shows, for example, the boy's sense of a lost mother haunting him at crucial times. The first awakening of the youth's senses is most astutely revealed. Meredith sees that he will be first stirred by the sentimental Lady Blandish who is a mother-figure; that next he will be shocked into the discovery of sensual love by seeing his father kiss Lady Blandish's hand. The irony will be that the boy is impelled into his first love affair by jealousy of the father who has been determined on his innocence. Much later on in the novel, when father and son, standing on their pride are refusing to make the first step towards a reconciliation, Richard's aunt warns him that his father will marry

Lady Blandish. It will cause a mild scandal for Lady Blandish lives in the house. The effect of this speech is surprising and adds something important to our knowledge of Richard's character. In Meredith's words:

> He pondered what his Aunt said. He loved Lady Blandish, and yet did not wish to see her Lady Feverel. Mrs Doria [the aunt] laid painful stress on the scandal and though he did not give his mind to this, he thought of it. He thought of his mother. Where was she? But most of his thoughts recurred to his father and something akin to jealousy slowly awakened his heart to him. He had given him up and had not latterly felt extremely filial; but he could not bear the idea of a division of which he had ever been the idol and sole object.

Although *The Ordeal of Richard Feverel* is a comic-tragedy about education, behind it is the strong theme of class-conflict. Richard's war with Farmer Blaize is a study in the landowner-yeoman-farmer struggle which is a very Victorian subject. Lucy is a simple country girl and therefore socially unacceptable. The class and education comedy is seen in the comic interview of Sir Austin with his lawyer, where the lawyer is condescended to and the lawyer's son Repton is caught hiding indecent books in his desk. Sir Austin's overt reasons for preserving his son's chastity are religious, moral, but above all social. He desires his class to be an impeccable sinless élite. In fact this has made the son arrogant in a high-minded way, strong-willed and a prig. Unlike, say, Tom Jones who merely commits follies, Richard is a sort of handsome anti-hero who is selfish, hot-tempered, and blinded by a youthful egoism disguised as principle. His pride is more forgivable than his father's and is relieved by the engaging, growing powers of youth.

Meredith is above all a novelist of youth and growth; for he accepts with pleasure the conceit, the severity, the aggressiveness and self-encumberedness of young men and women, the uncritical impulses and solemn ambitions. Their follies are undertaken with passionate single-mindedness. To my mind only Tolstoy and Stendhal really succeed in portraying young men because they understand and admire egotism; that is Meredith's interest, too, and it gives his young men something in common with Stendhal heroes above all. The secondary character, Repton, the lawyer's son, with his follies and muddleheadedness, his sentimentality and fits of libertinism is much closer to the conventional, sanguine young man in the English novel from Tom Jones to Lucky Jim. He is very well-drawn. But because Richard is deeply class conscious and sees himself as a leader, purifying society of its evils, he is made to become aware of another ideal: it is one that Meredith learned from his education by the Moravians —a belief in the guidance of nature and in human brotherhood.

The Ordeal of Richard Feverel shows henceforth what Meredith will contain and the methods he will use. First, the novel will have an essay-like frame, enclosing set scenes. The essay will carry the narrative forward. Obviously Peacock must have taught him something here. The essay-like form will help him in his greatest difficulty as a writer: how to pull together his conflicting interests. He is a poet, a symbolist who must be lyrical; lyrical, he must also be comic, moving from the comedy of manners to the grotesque; there is the social satirist; there is the man of fantasy; there is the realist. And there is the man who has ideas about the state of England; there is the wit and artist who feeling deeply for Nature as a headlong Force yet identifies it with the sanity Comedy teaches us—a not impossible but very difficult conjunction of ideas. As he sees it, the extraordinary mixture can be made to look coherent by the skilful use of styles and by a new view of narra-tive. Narrative can no longer be a straightforward, chronological arrangement of stirring events in an exciting plot. It must first be oblique. The exciting *scène à faire* need not be faced. It can be foreshadowed, rumoured, evaded, commented on by the guesses of several different witnesses afterwards. Climax may be conversation. No one will quite know what happened and though the reader may be maddened the suspense is thereby increased. And anyway it is like life. Time is open, as it was to become for novelists like Proust, Virginia Woolf and Ford Madox Ford. Meredith put his case in these words in one of his digressions to the reader in the course of the book:

At present, I am aware of an audience impatient for blood and glory that scorns the stress I am putting on incidents so minute, a picture so little imposing. An audience will come to whom it will be given to see the elementary machin-ery at work; who as it were, from some slight hint of the strains, will feel the winds of March when they do not blow. To them nothing will be trivial, seeing that they will have in their eyes the invisible conflict going on around us, whose features a nod, a smile, a laugh of ours perpetually changes. And they will perceive, moreover, that in real life all hangs together: the train is laid in the lifting of an eyebrow, that bursts upon the field of thousands. They will see the links of things as they pass, and wonder not, as foolish readers now do, that this large matter came out of this small one.

As he said in *Modern Love* "passions spin the plot". That is to say plot is a *web* and not a mechanism. So, we do not *see* Richard actually burning the rick when he is a boy. We know only because he is caught gleefully watching the glow from his bedroom window; and through Adrian, his tutor, who is observing the boy, listening to his conversation and guessing what is going on. The secret wedding of Richard and Lucy is the centrepiece of the comedy and it is brilliantly handled. We have the comedy of Richard evading his ludicrous Uncle Hippias in London, of Repton finding lodgings for Lucy, the portrait of the sentimental landlady who doesn't know at first who the lovers are, of Richard's touching meeting with Lucy who is afraid until he utters the word "husband". There is the comic suspense when, on his way to his secret wedding, Richard is nearly thwarted by an unlucky meeting with Mrs Doria and her daughter in the Park. He is nearly caught out and, in his confusion, he drops the wedding ring and loses it. This small incident is piquant, for Lucy has to borrow her landlady's ring. It is a passing humiliation that brings out the obstinacy and stamina in the pretty girl, now that she realises she has burnt her boats. The tipsy behaviour of young Repton afterwards is an excellent anti-climax. Adrian discovers the rendezvous too late. He confronts the landlady and here a less ingenious novelist might have taken us straight to the showdown with Sir Austin:

but Meredith contrives a new delay. When Adrian sees the wedding cake on the landlady's table it becomes both a symbol and an instrument for causing comic trouble. He wraps a piece up and takes it round to the other members of the family and duly waits for them to guess its significance. This is high comedy; the sight of the cake stirs everyone in his own way. And it is particularly good that the scene proceeds slowly, for in comedy the pace must be slowed down, savoured in detail at the climax—in such matters Meredith is a master who knows how to squeeze every drop of irony out of it. Comedy depends always on seeing the same event or idea over and over again, in different lights. Meredith knows, for example, he can afford to delay matters even more by going into Adrian's motives for taking the cake off. It will be dramatic, he will enjoy the general wonder, he will be making fools of the family; but there is something else:

> "So dies the System" [is Adrian's comment as he leaves Mrs Berry's]. "And now let the prophets roar! He dies respectably in a marriage-bed which is more than I should have foretold of the Monster." Meantime, he gave the Cake a dramatic tap: "I'll go sow nightmates".

And then, as Fielding would have done, Meredith opens the next chapter with an ironical study of Adrian as a blackmailing parasite on a rich patron.

The last act of the wedding comedy must be in the mind of Sir Austin and here Meredith is masterly in another way. He knows that the manner must change and that Sir Austin's state of mind must now be at the centre of the scene. Almost any other novelist expert in direct narrative would have shown us young Repton

arriving scared at the great house to confront Sir
Austin with Richard's letter announcing the marriage
and begging his forgiveness, and waiting for the storm.
Meredith refuses this scene. What he always seeks is a
symbol first. And here the symbol is the speechlessness
of Repton. He cannot speak because he is drunk. He
lies snoring out a hangover on the couch before Sir
Austin's freezing eye. Repton, the non-ideal, the wild-
oats sower! Is this what the world believes in? Again,
Meredith perceives that a man so rigid in idealism as
Sir Austin is, will be rigid in despair. His sanity will
make him increase the *area* of despair; it cannot, for
him, be less than global. Meredith says:

> For a grief that was private and peculiar, he unhesitatingly
> cast the blame upon humanity; just as he had accused it in
> the period of what he termed his own ordeal. How had he
> borne that? By masking his face and he prepared the ordeal
> of his son by doing the same.

The terrifying thing about Sir Austin is that he has no
anger. He believes in the "Spartan comfort of bearing
pain and being passive". And, of course, his subsequent
cruelty, his cat-and-mouse treatment of Richard, is the
outcome of the sado-masochist's passivity.

After this the brilliant book ceases to be a comedy
and, in fact, we lose our sympathy for Richard and,
even for Lucy. Meredith is relying on his powers of
contrivance which are considerable, but the incredible
is being contrived. His Idea now distorts his characters,
instead of filling them out. The aphorisms which were
meant to act as side-wings to the stage set now fail to
contain it and become tiresome. It is arguable that
Lucy and Richard ought to die in accordance with the

Romeo and Juliet motif and that Sir Austin and Adrian (the Wise Youth) should be seen as miserable but impervious little pedants. We are shocked to see that Richard is as *entêté* as his father for we had, excusably, been carried away by Meredith's earlier Romantic portrait and we shall recall it again when we come to *Beauchamp's Career*. But the psychological point is made. Meredith was clever about Richard's duel and Mrs Mount's confession but it does seem that here there was a concession to the blood and glory school, to the melodramatic. The death of another girl who had loved Richard in vain is surely an unnecessary complication. It is put there, of course, to show that the World's idea of marriage is as bad as the System's. The novel does not end in tragedy, but in general bitterness unpurged. An ugly clownish grimace is left. We recall Henley's remark about Meredith holding the pen of a great artist in one hand and the razor of a spiritual suicide in the other.

The weakness of intensely personal novels is that they do not wholly transfigure the personal experience. It is well-known that *The Ordeal of Richard Feverel* is very much an autobiographical novel. It was inspired, as I said earlier, by two fathers—his own and by himself as a father. He wrote it in the bitter period when, deserted by his wife for another man, he poured an overwhelming amount of love upon the son he was left to bring up. As shadows, his wife and her lover appear in the novel; so that we are blatantly invited to see that under the comedy there is an unresolved torture and that real life is grimacing unassimilated. It is as though here the actor forgot to put on his paint.

Like all novelists, Meredith drew his characters from life, but the general practice is to mix oneself, one's idea, with the portrayed person; and after starting off, the novelist is almost certain to combine several models in one. If one starts, say, with a real bully, one very soon adds bits of other bullies to him, for the novelist knows that until reality has been made unreal, it is not real in art. Meredith, in his egotistical way, was apt not only to take characters from real life, but often read his accounts of them to the models who approved or criticised. This does not necessarily show great delicacy or discretion; rather it seems to indicate that as far as the romantic egoist was nonchalantly concerned, they were not real people to begin with. Only *he* was real.

Chapter Four

Chapter Four

THE desire for the fulfilment of a romantic foreign self is at the heart of the Meredith notion of the Ordeal. In one book the hero is successful, in a dubious way; but this book, *Evan Harrington*, is no more than a passable autobiography. It follows the story of the Meredith family very closely. The grandfather, the fantastic old Mel who gallivants among the gentry, famous everywhere for his wit, his love affairs, his extravagance, is dead at the beginning of the novel. This, in a sense, contracts it: the lazy-minded Meredith is content with hearsay. Mel's son comes home from Portugal where an aunt has married a Portuguese diplomat and has consorted with the aristocracy; the youth's head has been turned and his heart captured, too, by the grand foreign society he has lived in; he now has to face his low English reality. He has to face the fact that he is the heir to a bankrupt shop and his father's debts. The boy is no more than the son of a "snip". His ambitious sister wants him to become a gentleman and a diplomat; his commanding mother convinces him that he must give up such nonsense, settle to work, pay off the debts and save the shop. The question is the burning Victorian question, one that lasted out the century from Dickens (*Great Expectations*) to Shaw, Wells, Ford and Maugham: What is a gentleman? It is the obsessive preoccupation of the ever-expanding middle class. In terms of the class war you have to show the gentry that you are more of a gentleman than any one of them really is. You have to show that you are *morally* superior. The word "gentleman" has lost its interest for us now; in the '30s it was replaced by another illusion: the moral superiority of the working class. Our obsession with class has seriously limited psychological penetration in the English novel, when one compares it with the American, the Russian or the French. "Placing" in society, for ambiguous moral reasons, has made us, (even more today,) eccentric and parochial.

We see Evan Harrington first of all giving up his romantic dream, agreeing to go back to tailoring; then, by accident, he again meets the aristocratic girl he has been in love with in Lisbon. Dreading to lose her he does not tell her his secret, plays the part of the gentleman beautifully in her grand house. He is eventually exposed; his mystified girl has to give him up; but, he has so impressed the wealthy man on whom the grand family depend, that he inherits their money —a good climax for the comedy. Here is the test: Evan gives the money back. That is to say, he is more of a gentleman, and a genuine one, than the gentry. At the last moment, the girl breaks her engagement to his rival, and he wins her.

Evan Harrington was a bid to make money. The plot, once its rambling beginning is over, is well-made. The satire at the expense of English snobberies is neat, and in aiming at the large public he wrote in a plain, humorous style and did not attempt the artificial staging of scenes. But without artifice Meredith is crude and thin. A novelist's virtues spring from the same roots as his vices. The worst thing in the book is in its borrowings from Dickens and here Meredith's bookishness is worse than an evil; it is shallow. Two characters, Cogglesby and Raikes are straight out of Dickens and so never belong to the scene. Meredith perpetuates the reach-me-down Dickensian character which has bedevilled later English novelists, and even more, their critics who suppose, as I said in my first lecture, that the comic characters of Dickens are oddities. Only one character in *Evan Harrington* escapes this limitation and that is Evan Harrington's sister, the so-called Countess who is married to a well-observed Portuguese diplomat. The reason why she is well-done is the reason for which one thinks any of Dickens's comics sound: she is living out a personal myth. Her absurdity is that she is a giddy snob who has romantically made good and is determined, by sheer will-power and resource—which are funny because they are inexhaustible—that Evan shall stop being a tailor and rise to the airy world she lives in. She is frequently shamed, set back, laughed at, but she is indomitable. One can say that she is dotty, that is to say she lives in an unreal world, but she has at any rate the power to preserve it for herself if not for others. She has a sort of inspired insensibility. And Meredith triumphs with her when he turns her, in the end, into a Catholic convert; driven into a corner, she says that no Protestant can be a gentleman. Only the Pope can do the trick. She writes to her sister:

> I *know* it to be impossible for the Protestant heresy to offer
> a shade of consolation. Earthy born it rather encourages
> social distinctions. It is the sweet sovereign Pontiff alone

77

who gathers all in his arms, not excepting tailors. Here if
they could know it, is their blessed comfort! . . . Oh! the
gentlemanliness of these infinitely maligned Jesuits.

This is something more than farce of the period.
Meredith is carrying the Dickensian soliloquist a step
further—towards his relation to social pressures and
the lure of a romantic idealism, poor but observable.
Quick, wounded and critical, Meredith was capable of
a psychological extension of the genuine Dickensian
character. He saw that the Countess had the courage
of her illusions and that she was a fantastic *exalté:*

> the misfortune of dear Papa's birth did not less enable him
> to proclaim himself *in conduct* a nobleman's offspring and
> that a large outfitter, one of the largest, was in reality a
> *merchant* whose daughters have often wedded nobles of
> the land and become *ancestresses.*

Her final words at the end of the novel give it the exact
yet extravagant tone that Meredith's comedy requires:

> I am persuaded of this: that it is utterly impossible for a
> man to be a *true gentleman* who is not of the true Church.
> What it is I cannot say; but it is as a convert that I appreci-
> ate my husband. Love is made to live, dear, for Catholics
> are human. The other day it was a question of whether a
> lady or a gentleman should be compromised. It required
> the grossest fib. The gentleman did not hesitate. And why?
> His priest was handy. Fancy Lord Laxley is such a case.
> I shudder. This shows that *your* religion precludes any
> possibility of being a *real* gentleman and whatever Evan
> may think of himself, or Rose think of him, I *know the
> thing.*

And there is a psychological point which indicates that
at the heart of the comedy there is a fine moral tussle

between the lovers. In the final love scene between
Evan and Rose, there is this interchange:

> "Evan! Why did you betray me?"
> "Betray you Rose?"
> "You said you loved me once."
> She was weeping and all his spirit melted and his love cried
> out. "I said 'till death' and till death it will be, Rose."
> "Then why did you betray me, Evan? I know it all. But
> if you blackened yourself to me, was it not because you
> loved *something* better than me? And now you think *me*
> false. Which of us two *has* been false?"

What was it he loved better? His *pride*, disguised as
probity.

That is a telling footnote to the class war.

But Meredith is only half himself when he is a realist.
He needs to cut the rope and float free; when he does
that he is able to see, as an artist must, his own reality
and to find his own seriousness. In range of character,
scene and complication, in execution and verve, in
seriousness, *Harry Richmond* is by far his most imaginative statement of the idea of the Ordeal. His obsessive
subject: the relation of father and son, the princely
dream and its bankruptcy, are here transfigured. He is
the master of his power of fantasy and he has as strongly
as Fielding and less sentimentally than Thackeray the
ironical sense of "the Way of the World". There is the
usual tiresomeness at the end of the novel. And the
rather Borrovian scenes with Kiomi and the gypsies
are lush and unappealing to us now; but given his
terms, the main substance of the comedy is bold and
fine. It is a great advantage that the book is written in
the first person. Percy Lubbock objected (in *The Craft
of Fiction*) that this was a defect because Harry Richmond

was prevented, as the narrator, from becoming as full a character as the dramatic conflict between father and son required. One has (he thinks) an impression of shadow-boxing. It is always tempting to write in the first person because of the instantaneous effect, because the method seems to carry the conviction of the first hand; it is nearly always good in adventure, in confession, and in novels in which—*David Copperfield* is an excellent example—the first person is mainly the observer of a wide scene, well-populated with characters. *Harry Richmond* has such a scene. But the first person can only guess what is in people's minds and he cannot directly know what people are doing when he is not there. The success of Dickens with this method in *David Copperfield* and *Great Expectations* owes a good deal to the fact that these novels begin with a boyhood and never quite lose the eager boyhood eye, when the narrator grows up. This eye of boyhood puts a distinction between him and the rest of the characters who have become adult and know the bewilderments and involvements of grown people. *Harry Richmond* also begins with the narrator's boyhood—and very well too—but the eye of a man is looking over his shoulder; and there is nothing boyish in Meredith. Here I differ from Percy Lubbock: one is left with a moving, pervasive portrait of Harry, a conscious self-portrait. Meredith was a natural first person writer. In the first place, as we know, he is a chronic intervener in his novels, in a very professional way. For example, excusing himself for showing a husband flirting with his sister-in-law, he intervenes, as the novelist persecuted by Mudies, with the words:

> My constant error is in supposing that I write for the
> wicked people who begot us.

And Meredith intervened continuously in his novels by
playing a sort of second lead as the Comic Spirit. The
style is hortatory, buttonholding and vocative; he
pretty well tells us that without his dazzling presence
as a conversationalist and essayist, there will be no
novel. The hero escapes Lubbock's criticisms because
he is seen growing, reacting, changing and is given a
lot to do. One effect of first person narration was to
simplify his prose and to allow him to distribute his
fantasy, instead of inserting it as a personal side show.
Harry Richmond glows with its speed of telling. As
for the well-known difficulty of describing what the
narrator cannot have seen or known, Meredith's ingenuity is equal to it. The very avoidance of such
scenes and the *scènes à faire*, enables him to convey the
comedy of rumour, conjecture, rival versions which not
only build up what is missing, but create a vivid,
impressionist picture of the society surrounding a
character. And although Harry Richmond himself may
from time to time be flat and passive as a character he is
generally brought into focus by his own life and by the
intense involvement with his father's wild actions.
Harry can only be said to be flat at the end of the book
after the total exposure of his father—flat of course
because he is too exhausted by his experience to cut
any figure.

The central idea of the novel has the right kind of
Romantic effrontery. Richmond Roy, the father,
claims to be a pretender to the English throne. Wild
and very plausible claims were not uncommon in the

nineteenth century and had a special relevance to what I called before the habit of colonising history. To claim the royal connection one must look royal and act royally. This requires histrionic powers, nerve, quick-thinking, knowing when to push forward and when to vanish; ostentation and secretiveness must alternate; and, of course, the whole adventure requires money. The son must have the royal idea implanted in *him*. Harry Richmond himself might have been happier as a valet. As a son Harry Richmond is his father's valet, his Gil Blas or Sancho Panza: Meredith's choice of model has been made with the acumen formed of a thorough knowledge of the tradition.

What is masterly in this novel is the way in which Meredith plants the royal delusion, at every changing stage, in Harry Richmond's mind and the reader's. The claim is allowed to blossom as a rumour, so that we scarcely notice that we have not been given anything concrete to go on. One is made to go into a trance. This trance would evaporate as we read, but for the symbolism which it contains: the novel is not simply an adventure, but a studied account, as Richard Feverel was, of an education. The book is a picaresque *Bildungsroman*. For young Harry Richmond is shown struggling with the conflict of the romantic and the positive or truthful spirits in himself; he is carried now one way and now the other, and he has to be shown in the end achieving self-mastery. He has to step out of his own egoism and master it. The surrounding characters in the novel are carefully and subtly placed so as to illustrate, without open preaching, the two points of view.

For the careless reader, the opening chapter might seem like a piece of melodramatic Wardour Street. That is to miss the subtlety with which the main theme of the book is insinuated. This is the fruit of Meredith's constructive power and above all his mastery of more than one prose style. You remember the banging at Squire Belton's door at two in the morning, the arrival of the handsome, cloaked Richmond Roy at the house demanding to see his wife whom he had abandoned and who in fact is shut up there and insane. The dialogue is in two languages—the forthright, Squire Westernish bluntness of the squire, and the theatrical High Romantic tone of Richmond Roy. The squire refuses to allow Roy into the house. He shouts:

> "And here's a scoundrel stinks of villainy, and I've proclaimed him 'ware my gates as a common trespasser, and deserves hanging if ever rook did nailed hard and fast to my barn doors."

Roy counters this in the high Lyceum manner:

> "A curse be on him, heaven's lightenings descend on him who keeps husband from wife in calamity."

The squire whistles up his dogs.

> "Now," answers Roy, "Now sir on your application during tomorrow's daylight shall I see her?"
> "Nor, sir, on your application"—the squire drawled in an uncontrollable mimicking contempt of the other's florid forms of speech, ending in his own style, "No, you wont".

Defeated by the squire, Roy cannot be prevented from taking off his four-year-old son into the night. End of chapter. But note this chapter is written in the third person by an omniscient narrator. Chapter Two: to our surprise the narrative is taken up in the *first* person by the son, which is essential to Meredith's scheme, and one sees how brilliant it is of him to have broken the continuity. The boy can have had only one source for the story of the incident—his father's romantic evocation of it afterwards; he has been entrapped by his father's story-telling, and will go on being so trapped, by his father's powerful imagination.

> "That night," Harry writes, "stands up without clear traces about it or near it, like the brazen castle of romance round which the sea-tide flows."

He hears more of the scene subsequently, from Sims the Squire's butler; it is a typical device of Meredith's to slip in hints or rumours—and they are dramatised: they are not explanations—about an event long afterwards. The father is a genius as an entertainer and teacher. He romanticises English history; he cunningly throws in high politics and literature—William Pitt and Shakespeare muddle the boy's mind. The boy has the confused impression that King Lear hunted deer, that Lady Macbeth steeped her handkerchief in the deer's blood and that Shylock ordered a pound of the carcase. This confusion is not simply a novelist's joke: everything in Meredith forwards his purpose. A man calls one day and after a brief row, the father introduces him to the son as "Shylock's great-great-great-grandson" and says that Shylock was satisfied with a pound but his descendant wanted 200 pounds or else his whole body. "My father went off with Shylock's very great-grandson arm in arm, exclaiming 'To the Rialto'."

It is our first hint that Richmond Roy is living by his wits and is being hauled off to prison for debt. The boy is left studying Burke's Peerage—as part of his education—and astonishes the landlady by being able to answer questions like "And who married the Dowager Duchess of Dewlap"?

The effect on the landlady and her friends is enormous:

> Gradually, [Harry says] my ear grew accustomed to her invariable whisper on these occasions. "Blood rile," she said and her friends all said "No!" like the run of a finger down a fiddle string.

In those few words the great effrontery that Richmond Roy is a pretender to the throne is cunningly domesticated in our minds.

We are now advanced into a comic adventure: Richmond Roy's fantasies revive, his claims are darkly revealed to the adoring son. The pair live in a grand London house, surrounded by flunkeys and portraits of royalty. Meredith's inventive fantasy is awake. There is a superb escapade when the father daringly orders a coach with scarlet livery. The money is said to come from influential circles; he conveys that he is playing off the British Government, who wish to keep him quiet, against the small band of rich supporters of his claim. The son adores the father the more because he is the victim of injustice.

But Meredith has now to introduce a new perception: the extraordinary life Harry is living makes him observant, and this eventually leads him to think he can see into people's secret minds. There is a small but marvellously well-timed moment, after the guests have left a rowdy dinner party when Harry notices "My father had fallen mournful". In a side glance like this,

Meredith has the power to lead us to a new inner development in the minds of his people and the direction of his tale. *We* know that Richmond Roy is a fraud; but by what stages will this reach the boy's mind? What will it do to him, as he grows? How will the wish to separate illusion from reality or to behave in both at once, be affected? If he is loyal, is it because his father has placed the delightful and deadly romantic infection in his character? He is disturbed because he notices his father's power over women and he is jealous; but—so far gone is the boy under the father's spell—the jealousy (Harry Richmond says):

> added a curious romantic tenderness to my adoration of him and made me feel he and I were against the world.

So, in the course of the novel, the fundamental theme is always enacted in the terms of the innumerable details of a living relationship between the people. As the boy grows the father is frank with him up to a point and these confidences are timed to follow the great scenes in the book.

It is important to show the boy secretly hoarding his father's glamour when, after one of the father's many *debâcles*, the boy returns to the squire's house and here is under the saner influence of the squire. The squire is his grandfather. Here, too, we run into the first conflict in love. Harry is headlong in friendship and always dreams of escape to London to find his father. He has no time for love of the sensible, obstinate sweet Janet whom the Squire wants him to marry; he is soon involved with Kiomi, the savage young gypsy beauty. She represents wild Nature, primitive but always honest in its own terms. This Borrovian episode shows us that

86

Harry is as self-willed as Richard Feverel was—again
Meredith is good about the blind self-will, the gener-
osity and the rather fine unquestioning conceit of youth.
The first great escapade takes him, by luck, to his
father in Germany. Harry and a cheerful school friend
called Temple get away to London and after a few
misadventures in the London streets, are kidnapped by
a Calvinist sea-captain. Having rescued them from
prostitutes, the Captain spends his time exhorting them
with prayer and Bible on the journey across the Channel.
Once in Germany, by one of those strokes of coinci-
dence permissible to Romance, he is put on the track
of Richmond Roy. The father is having the time of his
life in a small German court where he has captivated a
bored margravine by his antics. The encounter with
the son occurs at the climax of one of the father's
exploits and here Meredith—always in love with
fantasy—startles by his power to make the fantastic
credible. After all, it is the central point of the novel
that the seemingly impossible must be made comically
possible. I am speaking of the statue scene, that has
annoyed some critics but which to my mind is beautifully handled. An equestrian statue is to be unveiled
and there we see the awe-inspiring bronze figure of the
Prince Albrecht on the horse. The band plays, the
crowd stares and the two impudent English youths give
it a school-boy cheer, in order to annoy the Germans.
At which the bronze statue turns its head:

I found the people falling back with amazed exclamation.
I—so prepossessed was I—I simply started at the sudden
flashing white of the statue's eyes. The eyes from being
an instant ago dull carved eyeballs, were animated. They

were fixed on me. I was unable to give out breath. Its chest
heaved; both bronze arms struck against the bosom.
"Richmond! My son! Richie! Harry Richmond. Richmond Roy." That is what the statue gave forth.

That is abrupt. So abrupt that Meredith may almost be
accused of funking not the scene, but the action in it.
But he at once makes the fantastic acceptable by
parcelling versions of it among several minds who
confirm it in different ways. This thoroughly implants
the fantasy and makes its texture richer. Then Meredith,
having now completed the task of convincing us, nips
the farce in the bud and goes to the boy's mind.

My head was like a ringing pan. I knew it was my father,
but my father with death and strangeness, earth, metal
about him; and his voice was like a human cry contending
with earth and metal—mine was stifled.

Meredith notes how Harry's mind works under the
shock

I became a perfectly mechanical creature; incapable of
observing, just capable of taking an impression here and
there; in such cases the impressions that come are stamped
on hot wax; they keep the scene fresh; they partly pervert
it as well. Temple's version is, I am sure, the truer historical
picture.

This is not a novelist's aside about the process of
observation, for note the phrase "they partly pervert it
as well". This phrase pushes the story forward, for
Meredith is beginning to point out that Harry's judgment of his father is leaving the simple adoring stage
and that his judgment will now begin to be perverted.

Meredith moves on to his favourite habit of building
a scene after it has happened. We turn to Temple's

version of the affair. This youth noticed that when Richmond Roy climbed down from the bronze horse he did not jump to earth in one bound, as Harry fancied, but clambered with difficulty and walked towards him "like a figure dragging logs at its heels". And Temple noticed one more thing: the petulant old margravine had her watch in her hand. (There is an absurd interval when Richmond Roy goes off with the boys to struggle out of his bronze-varnished, metallic-looking disguise.) In a page or two we shall know why the margravine has her watch in her hand: Richmond Roy's imposture was done for a bet and she bursts out into a fish wife's tirade because Richmond Roy broke the conditions. In fact, he surpassed them. He said he had stipulated for fifteen minutes on the horse; he sat it out for twenty-three. The moral is that, only by living in a Court can the son (who is going to become a prince) learn the exigence and capriciousness of princes. And so we come to the next stage in the development of those who live by romantic delusion; they may degenerate into mountebanks. The son is torn between loyalty to his father and the powerless knowledge that his father is no more than a pathetic court jester to a bored old princess. Harry's role as powerless observer is part of his own corruption. He notes that his father

took the colour of the spirits of the people around him

and

So conversational were his eyes and brows that he could persuade you to imagine he was carrying on a dialogue without opening his mouth. His laughter was confident, fresh, catching, the outburst of his very self, as laughter should be.

but its effect fades at once when he goes out of a room even for a moment:

> Strange to say, I lost the links of my familiarity with him when he left us on a short visit to his trunks and portmanteaux.

After the German adventure, Richmond Roy turns up at Bath pursued by an heiress and Harry joins him in the comedy and, having got money out of Squire Belton, temporarily pays his father's way. We now see something terrible: that the father's love of his son is as false as everything else about him; he is really after the fortune the son will inherit from the Squire. In Bath, Richmond Roy is in danger of what he most fears: marriage. He slips away.

Harry Richmond deludes himself now with the notion that his father is the victim of circumstances and is not an impossible character. The spell of his talk still works, even if his actions appal:

> I may call it a thirsty craving to have him inflating me, puffing the deep unillumined treasure-pits of my nature with laborious hints, as mines are filled with air to keep the miners going.

A laborious metaphor, it is true, but the conclusion is exact: passivity leads to the loss of any sense of value.

> While he talked he made these inmost recesses habitable. But the pain lay in my having now and then to utter replies. I found a sweetness in brooding unrealizingly over dreams and possibilities, and I let him go gladly that I might enjoy a week of silence, just taking impressions as they came, like the sands in the ebb tide.

The son knows his father's methods of persuasion are subtle and allows himself to be deceived; when they are back in Germany and Harry is in love with Ottilia, the princess, the father encourages the boy by "the veiled method". It was, as one knows, the method Don Quixote frequently used with Sancho.

Richmond Roy has sometimes been called another Micawber; an example of the weakness of English critics for calling all strange and histrionic characters Dickensian. But compared with Roy, Micawber is only half a character. Dickens did not present the dark and rascally side of the Micawberish character; if the comic gift is poetic Micawber is a figure in popular poetry. He is more exact in outline than Roy, but he is not an idea as well as a man; neither the man nor the idea is analysed. Micawber is never a tragic figure, but to some extent Roy is. Micawber waits for something to turn up; Roy, the rogue, makes it turn up. Micawber is possibly curable. Roy is incurable, will exhaust himself, will die. He will affect everyone; Micawber affects no one except Mrs Micawber. David is never seriously involved with him. Micawber derives his body from the general London fantasy; Roy has no scene; but when he appears he creates one. He is floating.

He infects Harry; he uses Harry, his son, just to get his money. He will exploit his heart for it. He pushes the impossible love affair with Princess Ottilia, for his own interests. And when at last, total bankruptcy, disgrace and exposure arrive, and he is reduced to the level of a joke, Meredith hits upon one of his most spirited pieces of invention. Good comedy depends a great deal on what one calls the doubling principle, either by repeating an episode in other circumstances or another key, or by introducing a character to his double. Since Meredith is expert in the fantastic and knows how to make it acceptable, the episode is marvellously successful. He confronts Richmond Roy with a false Dauphin, a claimant to the French throne. The incident is also one more example of the merits of avoiding the *scène à faire*. This is how he builds it. He begins by stating the confrontation with the double as a rumour. Success depends on the complexity, the gaiety and suggestiveness of the surrounding events. Briefly, the father is giving splendid Balls in London announcing the forthcoming marriage of Harry to Ottilia—which is scandalously untrue—in short, creating one of his social mystifications, in the interests of his claim. Suddenly Squire Belton picks up the rumour about the Dauphin. The hearsay is put into the mouth of the choleric squire who is dining *en famille*. He is always a good narrator:

> "I tell you they call him Mr I K Dine in town. Ik Dine and a Dauphin. They made a regular clown and pantaloon o' the pair, I'm told. Couple o' pretenders to Thrones invited to dine together and talk over their chances and show their private marks. Oho! by-and-by William. You and I".

The ladies take the hint and retire. The squire continued in a furious whisper:

> "They got the two of them together, William. Who are you? I'm a Dauphin; who are you? I'm Ik Dine bar sinister. Oh! says the other, then I take precedence over you. Devil a bit, says the other; I've got more spots than you! Proof, says one. You're first, t'other. Count, one cries. T'other sings out Measles. Better than a dying Dauphin, roars t'other; and swore both of 'em was nothing but Port wine stains and pimples! Ha! Ha! And, William will you believe

it?—the couple went round begging the company to count the spots—ha! ha!—to prove their birth. Oh Lord, I'd ha' paid a penny to be there. A Jack of Bedlam Ik Dine damned idiot—makes name of Richmond stink!"

(Captain Bulstead shot a wild stare round the room to make sure the ladies had gone)

Worse: Richmond Roy had stood up at a public dinner and returned thanks on behalf of an Estate of the Realm. The last frightful news is conveyed in Meredith's most seeming casual manner to Harry while he is playing Badminton. It is over and over again the novelist's method to describe one action in the midst of another, simply because life as it is lived is in the intermingling of one surface with another. How does bad news come? What is the instant like? Harry hears it and in the same split second sees the beauty of Janet Ilchester's eyes as she raises them to volley back the shuttlecock. This is a treatment of action which the next generation of novelists will learn and teach the cinema.

After this a much milder and subtler account than the squire's is given of the Dauphin-Roy meeting; the farce was not as broad as it was said to be. Farce, *in reality*, rarely is—Meredith notes. And he wishes to show that even in ridicule Roy could hold to some taste and dignity. How else could his career be credible? So, yet another account comes from the fomentor of the plot. There are three indirect accounts, three turns of the screw; they make the whole fantastic incident settle into reality and they make it more diverting than a single straightforward statement would do.

The climax of the novel has one of those surprises

that justify and give a solid and yet ironical foundation to a romance into which we had been willingly bounced. The rope, as Henry James would have said, had seemingly been absolutely cut by Richmond Roy's extravagant career. We have seen that he has got hold of his son's inheritance which has paid for the yachts, the chateaux, the town houses and parties, and his exploits at the German court. Now every penny has gone. Only one thing remains for Richmond Roy: to marry a wealthy merchant's widow in order to pay his colossal debts. The law threatens.

Here we must look at the women in the story. Meredith is a fervent admirer of women. He sees them idealistically and romantically at first: in each one he sees the captivating personal and moral essence; he is aware of them as persons who have minds, loyalties and dreams. They are moral entities, as well as being objects of desire. They want or have wanted to "become something"; they have conceived a future which contains something else besides their probable marriages. Meredith is deeply sensitive to a woman's longing to "become". Women know the *kind* of love they want. Trapped by their own weaknesses or by convention in an inferior status, they are not self-deceived. They are often idealists who keep their secrets and are devious. Their characters change and develop. It may be a criticism that there are no unpleasant or devilish women in his novels, despite his references to the serpent of passion. Some critics have seen Ottilia, the exquisite German Princess with whom Harry is in love as no more than a poetically idealised *princesse lointaine* and that a hidden Meredith is morbidly subject to the "romantic agony". Ottilia is undoubtedly a *princesse lointaine* to Harry, the romantic dreamer. But she is a realist. And she is what her education has made her. For example, Richmond Roy spreads the cunning rumour that Harry has been wounded by a would-be assassin. She rushes to his bedside. She is rather put out to discover that he has merely been wounded in a duel. Only a duel! She is a conventional princess. What a come-down! Everyone who is anyone in Germany has fought a duel at some time! So Romantic love ends and turns into a protective affection and becomes—in Meredithian terms—a platonic spiritual adviser, a piece of poetry that will remain in the mind as a guide in the later crises of life. But Ottilia will still be a conventional German princess, as well as a symbol. Against Ottilia must be put Kiomi, the gypsy, a primitive, and Janet, the decent practical girl who is real because she is difficult. We are made to unsee the women as dreams, and come to see them as they are and what they represent.

Yet how mad women can be! Harry Richmond's Aunt Dorothy gives us a tremendous surprise. Aunt Dorothy has done all she can to cure Harry's obsession; and Aunt Dorothy has stood everything. But when Harry sees that the only escape for his father (now that he is ruined) is to marry a rich woman who is a simpleton, the Aunt who is the sister—remember—of Richmond Roy's dead wife, is indignant at such an immoral proposal. The rogue has already driven one woman out of her mind. But is Aunt Dorothy's moral indignation genuine? Is she perhaps jealous? Indeed she is. All women are mad about Richmond Roy and she was and is the maddest. It is she (the squire discovers) who has secretly financed a great deal of Richmond Roy's career. It is she who secretly pays his creditors in the final disaster. Both sisters have loved the man. And—for in Meredith there is always the final irony—up to now Richmond Roy has always known whom he will swindle next and how he will do it: but now we learn he has no idea that Dorothy has loved him and has paid. That revelation destroys him: he has to face his reality; he is what he always was— nothing but a swindling, seducing music teacher and an emptiness. The end of Richmond Roy is a collapse into feeble-mindedness and insanity.

This ought to be the end of the novel, but, alas, Meredith adds tedious and unbelievable complexities and a final melodrama. He tries to show Harry recovering from the spell. I am afraid it does not convince. I don't think Meredith was convinced. It is, no doubt, tremendously symbolical that Harry should come home to see the family house burned down and his father burned alive in it, but it is too tremendous. Never trust a Victorian when he sets fire to a mansion at the end of a book.

Chapter Five

Chapter Five

WHEN we come to *Beauchamp's Career*, *The Egoist* and *Diana of the Crossways*, Meredith enlarges the implication of his study of romantic egoism, its gestures and its poses. With his foreign eye, he looks at England and finds that egoism is the dominant sickness of English society. Self-interest, self-complacency, self-love, self-righteousness are the characteristics of the Victorian islanders. The idea does not originate with him, of course—in politics he was some sort of Tory-Radical, an appealing English contradiction, very useful to the mid-Victorian novelists who unfailingly swing to a middle position. The idea originates with Carlyle who had written in *Past and Present* that "enlightened Egoism, never so luminous, is *not* the rule by which a man's life can be led . . . the soul will have to be rescued from asphyxia". And Meredith makes an ironic bow to Carlyle early in *Beauchamp's Career*. There is always a sad, intelligent, bullied widow forced to live in an ambiguous stituation in Meredith's novels, a mother surrogate. In this novel she is Rosamund Culling. She reflects on the hero, young Beauchamp, whom she adores as if he were a son:

His favourite author was one writing of Heroes, in (so she esteemed it) a style resembling either early architecture or utter dilapidation, so loose and rough it seemed, a wind-in-the-orchard style, that tumbled down here and there an appreciated fruit with uncouth bluster, sentences without

99

commencement, running to abrupt endings and smoke, like waves against a sea-wall, learned dictionary words giving a hand to street-slang, and accents falling on them haphazard, were slant rays from driving clouds; all the pages in a breeze, the whole book producing a kind of electric agitation on the mind and the joints. . . . To her the incomprehensible was the abominable, for she had our country's high critical feeling; but he, while admitting that he could not master it, liked it.

The religion of the egoist is Comfort of mind. It is this Comfort or complacency that has stupefied England in its enormous wealth and power, and has made the ruling classes indifferent to the masses and either torpid or hypocritical about social justice. *Beauchamp's Career* has two excellent portraits: one is Everard Romfrey (who doesn't like it that the workers pronounce the name as Rum Free). He is one of Meredith's wealthy Saxon squires with money in land and Welsh mines. He eventually becomes an Earl, a lazy, choleric, half-naïve, half-genial, cunning man whose faith is in the family blood and the preservation of game. He is a sort of prize bull but an eccentric. In Meredith's words:

a noticeable gentleman, in mind a medieval baron, in politics a crotchety Whig. . . . At one time a hot Parliamentarian, calling himself a Whig, called by the Whigs a Radical, called by Radicals a Tory and very happy fighting them all round.

His ancient family

had the root qualities, the prime active elements, of men in perfection, and notably that appetite to flourish at the cost of the weaker, which is the blessed examplification of strength. . . . Strength is the brute form of truth.

(Meredith's romantic attraction to Darwinism is mixed in with his irony.) Whatever may be said against Romfrey, he represents Nature but not Nature as Romantic poets such as Meredith think of it; it has nothing to do with moonlight, the North Downs, the sunrise. Nature is the breeding of animals, the facts of the fields, a countryman's stoical submission to natural law.

His chief opponent is Dr Shrapnel, the intellectual, firebrand Radical. The action of the book leads to a crisis in which a wild, long letter of Dr Shrapnel's is filched from Nevil Beauchamp, Romfrey's nephew. Dr Shrapnel tears the landed gentry and the manufacturers to pieces and urges young Beauchamp to political agitation. He is urging the young aristocrat to turn against his class:

> The religion of the vast English middle class is Comfort. It is their central thought; their idea of necessity; their solecism. Whatsoever ministers to Comfort, seems to belong to it, pretends to support it, they yield their passive worship to. Whatsoever alarms it they join to crush. They will pay for the security of Comfort.

And Dr Shrapnel storms on:

> The stench of the trail of Ego in our history. Trace the course of Ego for them . . . first the King who conquers and can govern. In his egoism he dubs him holy; his family is of a selected blood, he makes the crown hereditary—Ego. Son by son the shame of egoism increases; valour abates; hereditary Crown, no hereditary qualities. The Barons rise. They in turn hold sway, and found *their* order—Ego. The traders overturn them; each class rides the classes under it while it can. It is Ego—Ego, the fountain cry, original, sole source of war. Now comes the

workman's era. Numbers win in the end: proof of
small wisdom in the world. Anyhow, with numbers
there is rough nature's wisdom and justice. With
numbers Ego is inter-dependent and dispersed; it is
universalised.

It is the fiery Dr Shrapnel who inflames Nevil Beauchamp with a passion to fight for social justice. A
comedy has begun and an examination of the egoisms
involved, and the end will be disaster and fatality.
Meredith's comedies are apt to end in a smash. He
does not rise to those levels where comedy and tragedy
mingle and awaken compassion.

Beauchamp's England is the south; the scene of un-
rest is the not very politically-minded city of Southamp-
ton. The real drama, of course, is in the north and that
has to be reported by hearsay. The debate, as in
Peacock's attacks on industrialism, child labour and so
on, is conversation and hot-tempered epigram about
Tories, Whigs and the Manchester manufacturers.
The suffrage is still limited; it extends to the shop-
keepers, but the workers are outside it. They are
shadowy primitives, a muttering tribal force never
really seen; though there is one very marvellously
emotive glance at them hanging anxiously round the
gates of Shrapnel's cottage when Beauchamp is lying
dangerously ill and raving in a delirium that can be
heard in the street. This is one of those very moving
moments when some of Meredith's people cease to be
managed fictions and take on the deep seriousness of
human beings. Dr Shrapnel's opponents, on all levels,
think of him as a red revolutionary, and popular
emotion is for repressing him, even by violence. The

uppers want him to be thrashed; the frightened lowers won't greatly mind if he is beaten up.

The political action is confined to a local election and contains an ingeniously reported account of Press smears and bribery, the despair of agents, and the humours of canvassing. Meredith is as good at getting at the ruling idea in minor characters as in the major ones. He picks out the woolly optimist, for example, the liberal shop keeper, a sort of Christian Scientist who says "I truly don't know what it is *not* to know happiness". "Then you don't know God," says Carpendike, the Calvinist cobbler like a voice from the cave. A remark important to the novel—one has to keep one's eyes open for Meredith's small pointers; the gallant, aristocratic, amateur, Nevil Beauchamp, rejects Carpendike's gloomy views, but responds secretly to the fanaticism. We shall see the romantic young man turn into a single-minded fanatic who will throw away his private heart for the human cause. His life will combine self-destructive rashness with the passionate pursuit of social justice. It will be also a blind search for brick walls against which he can strike his head. Nearly all the characters of the book have an ingrained obstinacy.

The women of the novel are drawn into the political argument. (All, except one, are rich: great wealth is the hydrogen that makes the Meredithian romance sail into space.) And here we come to the heart of Beauchamp's career: he is divided about women. They are all enchanted by his person and by his chivalry; but chivalrous men are chronic rescuers. He not only wants to rescue the poor, but he also takes time off—in the middle of an Election, too!—to go over to France and rescue Renée, an aristocratic French girl who had once turned him down, from a bad, arranged marriage. (Like Shrapnel he believes arranged marriages are immoral.) Rescue and passion go together in him. He is defeated in this French adventure; he is defeated in the Election; he fails to get the rich English girl whom he has also painfully tried to rescue from her reactionary political views and family. He is paralysed when it comes to the conflict between passion and duty, ends in a brief dull marriage and dies by casual accident. Ordeal and defeat.

The fact is that Beauchamp, the enemy of the Ego, is passionately self-willed and self-absorbed. (He is innocently astonished when at the Election his opponents spread the rumour that he has crossed the Channel to see a French mistress.) He is also astonished that this mission arouses jealousy in the rich English girl he has been trying to reform. But, worse than this, when both relationships reach a crisis, he seems secretly to insure himself against either of his loves by putting his Cause —and also propriety—first: one notices that the typical Meredith hero is always involved with four women. For there is Shrapnel's daughter and also a mother-figure.

We have seen in all Meredith's novels that the ordeal quickly reaches the stage when the hero feels himself to be a crusading knight; in Beauchamp's case the crusade is made dramatic by its involvement in a personal loyalty to Dr Shrapnel. The large question of social justice is crystallised in his determination to see a murderous injustice to Dr Shrapnel put right. Beauchamp has been a naval officer: he will go to any lengths to rescue a comrade.

The double theme gives the drama its complexity. It brings out Meredith's power as an analyst of states of mind, and his gift for slipping out of one mind into another. As a Radical, Beauchamp is at war with his rich relations and Meredith brilliantly moves from the first skirmishes to the central battle. This battle has two main phases and both show his mastery of the discursive method: that is to say of narration by the back and forth shifts of commentary—a method which will be taken up later, as I have said, by Ford Madox Ford. Another novelist would either have shown us Dr Shrapnel at the hustings making a speech; or he would have shown him in some fierce political confrontation; or he would have simply printed Dr Shrapnel's explosive letter, and then shown progressively the stages of the row that it causes. Meredith takes another line. His whole aim as a novelist is to concentrate; and to split his conflicts among the hours of life as it goes by. So, the only times we see Dr Shrapnel are the off-stage moments, casually, not as a fighter but as a crankish domestic figure. In this way we are made aware of the contrast between Shrapnel as the slander says he is and as he really is. This is important because Beauchamp will know Shrapnel as he is—a decent English crank—and the others will know him only as a bogy.

This is made clear in Meredith's brilliant handling of the business of the violated letter. It is read aloud, in Romfrey's drawing room, by Baskelett, a cynical and pompous rival political candidate, to a company that includes the chief characters. Baskelett reads, indeed acts the letter out, to make it sound criminal and ridiculous; the reading provokes indignant but also comical reactions. Obviously Squire Romfrey ought to think the letter abominable; but his vanity can't resist Dr Shrapnel's note on the historic egoism of Barons! In general, the reading is a success but not the total success Captain Baskelett was looking for. In denouncing Shrapnel, he exposes his own shadiness and absurdity. The whole episode is beautifully done. The novel has come to life.

The second phase of the battle is far more serious. What has begun in mockery, now becomes grim. There is a comic scene in which Baskelett tries to provoke the doctor. He fails. The enraged Baskelett now persuades himself and Romfrey that Shrapnel has made insinuations about the status of the lady of Romfrey's house, Rosamund Culling, a widow who acts vaguely as his housekeeper and whose situation— in local opinion—is a matter of gossip. The hot-tempered squire who has himself quietly bullied the lady for years, marches down to Shrapnel's cottage and thrashes the old man within an inch of his life. This is the great shock of the novel. It is—to our ears, at any rate, unbelievable; it is certainly horrifying. But Meredith does not show us this crucial scene and this seems to me to show, for once, the weakness of his obsession with building up important things by hearsay and retrospect. Although he has got some of his best effects in this way, we see that he is a novelist whose dislike of confrontations can be evasive—in fact a fear of reality. Yet—was it fear? Pictorially vivid, intellectually subtle, he is impatient, perhaps lazy and even bored by a confrontation between author and fact. His originality lies in rejecting realism and parcelling events out among many people's minds.

Meredith could argue that his circuitous method here will make the violence of Beauchamp's reaction all the stronger. He wants to bring the moral issue forward. He has got to show the difference between people who simply act on unquestioned impulse and those who have a real conscience. Beauchamp will now never let his uncle, the squire, alone until he has forced him to apologise and nothing short of an earthquake will do that. One can imagine that other novelists would eagerly introduce such an earthquake, bringing Romfrey to his knees in remorse; but not Meredith. It is astonishing how free Meredith is of characteristic Victorian melodrama.

The subtle contriver has more plausible methods and turns to a study of the women in the book. What eventually brings Romfrey, now the Earl of Romfrey, to his knees, very briefly, is that he is manœuvred into marrying the widow, who becomes pregnant. The childless Earl is agog for an heir and is terrified that his wife—who is rather old for bearing a child—will miscarry; she adores Beauchamp and when she hears that he is at death's door in Shrapnel's cottage, she nags at her husband to make the apology. She is a blackmailer in love; the Earl tries to cheat but fears to cheat too much. Once again, comedy, but a true analysis of the situation, and at the point of death. There is an almost bizarre moment, when the widow guesses the Earl's pride is hardening up again and leading him to cheat by pretending he has apologised. She is bed-ridden and sends him a warning telegram. It is an absurd telegram, being partly in exalted Victor Hugo French, but it has an hysterical force coming from this dull woman who has endured much and now wakes up and puts on a great act. The telegram is a *coup de théâtre;*

> *Ni espoir, ni crainte, mais point de déceptions.*
> *Lumière. Ce sont les ténèbres qui tuent.*

Allowing for the exaltation, the appeal for spiritual honesty might have come out of Forster, say out of *Howards End.* Always connect or there will be panic and mess. Meredith's novels always move from one moral revelation to the next time. They move inwards.

Like Gissing, Meredith is remarkable for his portraits of women. They are delightful at first sight and as their portrayal continues they become more complex and more spirited. He is aware of how women see themselves; if *he* gets rather lyrical he admires both *their* self-idealisation and their conflict with their condition. He sees the essence of any woman's nature and its potentiality. As a feminist, he hated the subjection of women; and in *Diana of the Crossways*, he shows us a female egoist putting up a fight in a man's world. (Of course, being pre-Shavian and no economist, he thinks they'll have to put up with subjection for some time to come.)

After Rosamund Culling, there is Renée, the young French lady, shadowy, rather a theory about Frenchwomen—Meredith loves to theorise about national character; but she can sparkle. She has enchanted Beauchamp in the fine Venetian chapter at the beginning of the book. She will have the courage to live completely only if she is conquered by a commanding gesture, at the right moment and *not* treated as an equal. Beauchamp, who believes, on principle, in the rights of passion, misses this point and makes the Puritan mistake of presenting his love as *an argument* for the rights of passion. She can see through *that* self-protective device. For a time anyway, she could have been his most fiery Radical follower. Cecilia Halkett, her English rival, could not have been more than a worried Radical. She would always want to reform *him*. She *nearly* gives in but hasn't the courage. She is torn between feeling and her education as an upper class girl. Naturally she looks dashing. Meredith liked comparing women to yachts and she is a yachtswoman, a sea-lover, very conscious of class, conventional, reserved, desperately tempted. But only tempted. She makes a very good *Portrait of a Lady*—English style. Meredith is good at the simple phrases that tell, the small decisive moments. Cecilia is torn between resentment and love:

> Cecilia saw him and could not step to meet him for trouble of heart. It was bliss to know he lived and was near. A transient coldness following the fit of ecstasy enabled her to swim through the terrible first minutes face to face with him.

She is struggling against her love for Beauchamp, and she reasons rather than feels. When her reason tells her that she does love and always has loved—

> pain fled, to prove her reasoning good; the flames devoured her gently; they cared not to torture, so long as they had her to themselves.

Not the language a modern novelist could use, but the perceptions are simple and true.

Her difficulty begins as opposition to his Radicalism. She will only have him on her own right-thinking terms. But when she first sees his devotion to Shrapnel she is astonished to find she covets that love. She is almost converted by Beauchamp but hesitates at the last moment. She is humiliated by a jealousy she cannot control—Meredith is always good about jealousy—and afraid of Beauchamp's single-mindedness. It is she, rather than the French lady, who is the coquette because she is high-minded: against her own will, she rejects Beauchamp, but:

> she obtained a sudden view of her allurement and her sin in worshipping herself, and recognised that the aim at an ideal life closely approaches or easily inclines, to self-worship.

Illusions about her superiority and distinction prevented her from loving single-mindedly or whole-heartedly. And later on we shall see her, when the Beauchamp affair is over, resuming her role as "the peerless flower of English civilisation", a perfectly cool English lady crushing all memories of the love and the humiliating jealousy she had felt. Meredith is remorseless.

> Since we cannot have a peerless flower of civilisation without artificial aid, it may be understood how it was that Cecilia could extinguish some lights in her mind and kindle others and wherefore what it was not natural for her to do she did. She had, briefly, a certain control of herself.

She is the female egoist, the victim of the English self-love and self-justification. She has been unable to meet either Beauchamp's exacting conscience or his love; and

Beauchamp too is divided between conscience and passion. Two possibly Great People have snuffed themselves out. And—this is Meredith's point—obedient to the ethos of their class.

The end of the book is abrupt and cruel. It ends in a pointless accidental drowning. Beauchamp dies rescuing a working class urchin who has fallen into the sea. The allegorical intention is sound enough; but the tragedy is too perfunctory. It is really only casualty. Once more one feels that Meredith suddenly felt the personal despair that comes to the brilliant talker. The rocket has exploded in a shower of stars; now we are left with the stick. It was his half-petulant, half-weary habit to get back at his many critics at some point in his novels and he does this in an often quoted passage of *Beauchamp's Career*:

> My people conquer nothing, win none; they are actual yet uncommon. It is the clockwork of the brain that they are directed to set in motion, and—poor troop of actors to vacant benches—the conscience residing in the thoughtfulness which they would appeal to.

And it is true that the psychological novel was a new thing. Henry James was only just being published in England. But if one looks back what strikes one (I have to repeat) is the power of evocation. It dazzles like an Impressionist painting in which every brush stroke tells and contains something germane to the whole. One can feel time passing in people's minds. A scene at sea, a few touching words in a drawing room, a hint drawn out by a view from its window, the revelation of a loving woman's plot, will make a page that glides as fast as thought.

There is a short passage in *Beauchamp's Career* which foreshadows his next book, *The Egoist*. Cecilia Halkett is in Rome and is shocked by the rich English tourists. As an aristocrat who has been a little indoctrinated by Nevil Beauchamp she gives a snobbish, mocking account—"foreign to her nature" (Meredith is quick to note) "mockery served to veil her dullness".

> An ultra-English family, composed, shocking to relate, of a baronet-banker and his wife, two faint-faced girls, and a young gentleman of our country, once perhaps a light-limbed boy, chose to be followed by their footman in the melancholy pomp of state livery.
> . . . "This is your middle class," she says, "What society can they move in, that sanctions a vulgarity so perplexing. . . . Immense wealth and native obtuseness combine to disfigure us with this aspect of over-ripeness not to say monstrosity. . . ."

In being snobbish Cecilia Halkett failed to penetrate far into the nature of the banker and his family. The banker and his family were imagining themselves publicly and were becoming a particular dream. This is, again, a natural Meredith subject: the death of heart and sense, in those who feed back a false public image into private life. It is the subject of *The Egoist*.

Sir Willoughby Patterne is a gentleman, a sort of Darcy in his pride in his family or House. He is rich. He is a snob. England, says Meredith, is over-full of such amateurs. They receive the education of princes. They do not go into public life or serve their country. Their allegiance is to themselves and their estates. A great number hunt the fox. They like sport. But Sir Willoughby is not a barbarian; for reasons of prestige (for he likes to condescend to the intellect), he is an amateur scientist. Sir Willoughby's aim is to be re-garded as the most civilised of men, the most excelling. His concept of high civilisation is that it is as detached from the world at large as an unassailable mountain peak. The view is both metaphysical and—solely in his own interests—practical. His name is an intended pun: he is the pattern of a sterile concept of the civilised life. Move him into D. H. Lawrence's generation and he will be the famous tree with its roots in the air. There is no doubt that he is an authentic character and a particularly English one for he has the peculiar native weakness for being a personage. His estate, his friends, his servants, and the women he falls in love with are mirrors in which he regards his own beauty and virtue. So that he is more than a gentleman; he is an idea *in excelsis*, a gentleman who has every moment to act out the part before an audience. What he cannot stand is loss of audience. To people who cross him he is lofty, cold and dismissive. His idealism is self-love. So, as a lover he is a Narcissus, who looks for absolute purity in women, absolute faith. In this department Meredith says of him:

> He was a Social Egoist, fiercely imaginative in whatsoever concerned him. He had discovered a greater realm than that of the sensual appetites.

In marriage, he looks for heirs who will ensure the status of the House; in love, unquestioning adoration.

Here Meredith has found his ideal subject, the chance to fulfil the requirements he laid down in his Essay on the Comic Spirit. What had eluded him so often was the discipline of a form that would make his disparate gifts consort: the romantic, the lyrical, the epigrammatic, the analytic, the grotesque, the fantastic and the histrionic, so that they melt together and do not fall apart into anti-climax and incredibility. He had found such a form in the great romantic adventure-narrative of *Harry Richmond* by following the lesson of Fielding. In *The Egoist*, he saw that he must be stricter; that the subject needed unity of place; and that his Idea would be most intensely seen if he went to the theatre, to Molière and Congreve, and gave his novel the artifice of a play. English Egoism, for him, must be a theatrical subject; because its imagination is theatrical. His rapid scenes must be stated, reversed, re-stated, reversed again, so that Willoughby—the pattern—could be examined from all angles. The theme is the egoist's ordeal. He must slowly be reduced in his pretensions and the comedy will lie in the ruthlessness he brings to his self-defence when he begins to lose. There must be no sight of the struggling outside world. The thing must not sprawl; it is the business of comedy, Meredith holds, to condense. And to be perfect, the women must be equal in brains to the men. For it is part of Meredith's didactic purpose to show that the woman who marries the perfect gentleman will be his prisoner and subject; his pride will be more important than her love.

As usual, we see Meredith opting for a theory and for examining people in connection with it; and this brings the disadvantage that Meredith himself will be talking all the time and he will seem dangerously like Sir Willoughby in person as Clara Middleton found him:

Miss Middleton caught her glimpse of his interior from
sheer fatigue in hearing him discourse of it. What he
revealed was not the cause of her sickness—women can bear
revelations—they are exciting: but the monotonousness.
He slew imagination.

As a novel *The Egoist* has the monotony of a work of
animated criticism and it can be objected that Sir
Willoughby is a "still" portrait moralised by an essayist.
But all Meredith's turns before the curtain about
Egoism are good, because there is really no curtain. We
see the important notion that Egoism is more than a
trait: it is a faith, is personalised and shown not flatly
but ironically in action in the following passage:

> Consider him indulgently: the Egoist is the Son of himself.
> He is likewise the father. And the son loves the father and
> the father the son. . . . Are you, without much offending,
> sacrificed by them, it is on the altar of mutual love, to filial
> piety or paternal tenderness.

Meredith's irony is less a moralisation than an intended
dramatic intrusion on the scene. He does not comment
from outside, but seems to stop the actors, come up on
the stage and show them what they are doing.

Meredith had two important strokes of luck in
writing this novel. He had the luck to think of the boy
Crossjay, the ardent, mischievous imp, to make him
work as a nuisance and also to give him a heart.
Meredith himself—one would suspect—had no adult
heart; perhaps the loss of his mother, or the disaster
of his first marriage, had killed it. But he retained a
young pre-adult heart, rather as Dickens did.

The most refreshing things in *The Egoist* after the
superb opening scene are the glimpses we have of

Crossjay's and Clara Middleton's tender attachment to each other—a boy of ten's feeling for a young woman not yet twenty. Crossjay is one of the most engaging young schoolboys in English romance, at any rate in a scene so restricted as a gentleman's park. And there is a very serious background to the portrait: he is caught between two hostile theories of education. Education is always in Meredith's mind: how are we to be trained and for what? Crossjay brings surprise, a young animal's spontaneity, the love of action, the tenderness of Nature on to the scene; and Meredith has seen that the role of the young boy in such a novel is not comic relief; he will be a necessary, unconscious, light-footed messenger, a Puck without knowing it, in a stiff intrigue. The boy also draws out the romping or roguish side of the young girl who is being dragged too fast into the marriage system, which is her fate; but he also makes her think. The attraction of all Meredith's women is that they think. It is delightful to see Clara Middleton getting the courage to think for herself; to think her way through Sir Willoughby's formidable armour, to think her way into not being carried off by de Craye, the Irish gallant, without ceasing to be amused by him. Her quickness will cheer up the moralising Whitford who, rather to our regret, she will marry. She brings in all the good scenes of the out-of-doors—the famous cherry blossom scene, the excellent flight in the rain to the railway station: Meredith at his happiest. She brings the balancing touch of nature to a comedy which is necessarily artificial; and in the final conflict with Sir Willoughby, Meredith gives her a conscience. I am thinking of the moment when, after he has been caught proposing to Laetitia before he is "off" with Clara, he escapes by the casuistry that he was merely proposing on Whitford's behalf. He hands her over to Whitford and this has been thought psychologically impossible. I do not think so for it is the essence of Egoism to deny that control has ever left one's hands. And the comic point is well made: Sir Willoughby is given the escape-clause by which he, perpetually self-centred, can save his face and tell the world that he arranged it all; but *she* knows she has won. And has won, moreover, on his ground. He has done what he has said he never does—broken his word; and in going through the proper forms of asking for release, shows him, not without irony, that she is morally more scrupulous. The twists of the comedy are fine, but they are opportunities for further observation.

The last two chapters of *The Egoist* are excellent and the end is not one of the suicides of his talent. He has to avoid the conventional happy-ending, although Clara will be allowed it, of course, and like so many of his lovers will have an energetic courtship in the Alps where, as he writes, "Sitting beside them the Comic Muse is grave and sisterly". For the rest of the cast things will not be quite so easy. He goes on in the final sentence:

> Taking a glance at the others of her late company of actors, she [the Comic Muse] compresses her lips.

Willoughby has to take a final lashing from his future wife's tongue, for Laetitia has suffered much; she is seen trying to purge herself of bitterness. She had been a beautiful, healthy young girl like Clara; now she is in poor health. The scene in so many earlier Victorian novels would have been one of high-flown dramatic challenge and surrender; but Meredith sees to it that we are genuinely moved by this hard-headed woman:

> "Privation [she says] has made me what an abounding fortune usually makes of others—I am an Egoist. I am not deceiving you. That is my real character. My girl's view of him has entirely changed; and I am almost indifferent to the change. I can endeavour to respect him, I cannot venerate."

It is rather too pat (I have often thought) to make Laetitia an Egoist also. And surely, you will say, here *is* another suicide, this ending in a loveless marriage. No, because Willoughby is given his due: once he has his way, he is generous and recovers some of his incurable glow and Meredith, with one of his customary intrusions as if he were wryly introducing his personal life into the story, says:

> But he had the lady with brains! He had: and he was to learn the nature of that possession in the woman who is our wife.

Our wife! Meredith's personal story can never quite be kept out. So many of the lacerating and penetrating passages seem to come with force from that: those describing Willoughby's jealousy which echoes the jealousy described in *Modern Love:*

> the lover who cannot wound has indeed lost anchorage; he is woefully adrift: he stabs air, which is to stab himself.

Some words must be said about Meredith's dialogue. Up to his time, the rule has been that the chief characters speak in the voice useful to the novelist, and the minor characters—particularly the comics and the lower classes, are given natural idiomatic speech. The exception is Jane Austen, that superb technician who commanded several kinds of dialogue—formal or literary or natural. Meredith's dialogue brings in the modern wave. It is brisk, abrupt, allusive and born to its moment, for he builds his novels out of moments. He goes in for catching natural talk in snatches in the big chapters of rumour, and also for rapid epigrammatic stage repartee. In these interchanges, for the most part, the characters use only his brains. This can be exhausting; but, at its best, it is nimble. There is one curious innovation which sends the reader forward to Ivy Compton-Burnett: a stylised, choruslike speech which is given to the chorus of two spinster aunts and Dr Middleton in *The Egoist*. I think the following talk is good:

"This," [says Dr Middleton], "shall be no lost day for me if I may devote the remainder to you."

"The thunder we fear is not remote," murmured one.

They took to chanting in alternation:

"We are accustomed to peruse our Willoughby and we know him by a shadow."

"No one will accuse Willoughby Patterne of a deficiency of manliness; but what is it? He suffers, as none suffer, if he is not loved. He himself is unalterably constant in affection."

"What it is no one can say. We have lived with him all his life and we know him ready to make any sacrifice; only, he does demand the whole in return. And if he doubts, he looks as we have seen him today."

"Shattered: as we have never seen him before."

In the final novels, *Diana of the Crossways* and *One of Our Conquerors* the Comic Spirit is in abeyance. Meredith ventured to the sympathetic study of two women who were the victims of sexual scandal. The moral stage thunder is silenced and we see the psychologist at work. But *Diana* has some high-flown stuff in it, and while he is very penetrating about Diana's mixed motives at the crisis, the famous missing conversation in the newspaper office is fatal to the full grasp of her character. It is a sound point that this reckless lady is sexually frigid. She is not to be compared with the devious lady in Trollope's *The Eustace Diamonds*. Meredith lacks shrewdness and this is what his subject required. *One of Our Conquerors* is a much subtler, more fully-played drama. The theme could be Jamesian: a rich financier's attempt to marry off his illegitimate daughter to a peer, in order to compensate the mother for sorrow in her loss of status and her guilt; whereas it is the mother who prefers integrity in sorrow to fulfilment by a *coup d'état*. It is maddening that Meredith could follow every fine thread of this moral dilemma yet sandwich it from time to time between some of his stickiest prose.

I come to the end of my struggles with the most perplexing of our novelists in the nineteenth century. I have said nothing of one or two early novels, like *Rhoda Fleming* or *Sandra Belloni* because in them his powers were not yet formed; and I have said nothing about very late novels like *The Amazing Marriage* or *Lord Ormont and his Aminta*, because they are little more than responses to the change in public opinion about what a novelist was allowed to say about marriage and love outside marriage. Meredith had suffered, as much as Hardy, from the aggressive prudery of his readers; indeed more, for he had radical views on this subject. But they were personal, too, and it can be said that his idealism—we must evolve so that we rise above our sensuality—makes him to some extent a co-conspirator with his public, for he was very bitter about the adultery of his first wife. He was a very divided man.

There is a great gulf between us and all the Victorian novelists. We have to read them, with a translator's effort, for compared with the Russian and the French, they are unique in their morality and—in many ways—parochial in their class-consciousness. In the last quarter of the century Meredith represents the start of a breakaway. The difficulty we are most conscious of is that he interpreted Romance almost exclusively in terms of High Life. To present the Superb, he turned to the almost ludicrously grand and rich. In the idealisation of High Life or the Romantic view of it, he is not alone: we shall find it in Hardy and even in Lawrence; and it has many motives. In creating an imaginary or artificial scene Meredith, as I have many times said, was freeing himself for psychological observation. No doubt he over-subtilises, but his people live in their imagination; it gives an ambience to their lives. They dwell in states of mind and heart, personal to them.

There is little doubt that Browning and Meredith felt Shakespearean longings: almost all the Victorians had them. In Meredith's case the avowed use of the theme of *Romeo and Juliet* or *The Tempest* makes the

Shakespeare complex plain. Superb people are required and prose that is tapestry. They must be imported from Illyria, with Shakespeare's handsome disregard of geography. It was as if Shakespeare could be manufactured. One has the strong suspicion that the Victorians thought Shakespeare an optimist and idealist because he set his plays in Courts among great people. But perhaps all Meredith was after was the practical advantage: he needs a given subject, a given frame that he can embroider. Rich in verbal imagination, he is impotent when it comes to creating something new out of life. He will embellish or investigate; to have originated a Tess of the D'Urbervilles would be beyond him. All his novels are either on the given subject of autobiography or on borrowed or adapted material: the most notorious, in his time, being *Diana of the Crossways*, and the story of Lasalle.

The master of contrivance is unable to originate great themes, for these can only be born out of a profound and grand moral concern. Meredith's moral range is too personal. It leaves people without interest once youth is over. So we find that Meredith's gift is that of the brilliant commentator and scene setters, rather than that of the greatest creative artists. He has the strong Victorian feeling for the spell of places— Venice, the Alps, the Channel, the Downs. Like James he is morally a tourist. His positive contribution is that, in our comic and romantic tradition, he is a storehouse of ways and means, a fine diagnostician in his field as a poet will be; and rather hard and intelligently merciless —which is refreshing in the nineteenth century. And if he looks askance at many pretended virtues, the virtues he preaches (and happily by implication) are truthfulness and fortitude in the romantic disaster. He is a hot-house stoic and perhaps we should look upon him, first and last, as one of the startling temperaments of a very temperamental age.

V. S. PRITCHETT was born in England in 1900. He is a short-story writer, novelist, critic, and traveler. His short-story collections have appeared in the United States under the titles *The Sailor and the Saint, When My Girl Comes Home* and *Blind Love and Other Stories.* Among his novels are *Mr. Beluncle* and *Dead Man Leading,* and *The Key to My Heart. The Living Novel and Later Appreciations* is a collection of critical essays, most of which appeared originally in *The New Statesman.* His memoir, *A Cab at the Door,* was published in 1968. He is now a director of this paper and has been a life-long contributor. He also contributes stories and articles to *The New Yorker, Encounter, Holiday,* and the *New York Review of Books.*

Mr. Pritchett's extensive sojourns in Europe, the Middle East and South America have lead to the writing of several books of travel, the most recent being *The Offensive Traveller.* His books *London Perceived* and *Dublin: A Portrait,* each with photographs by Evelyn Hofer, have been widely acclaimed on both sides of the Atlantic.

Mr. Pritchett has visited the United States, where he gave the Christian Gauss lectures at Princeton, was Beckman Professor at the University of California in Berkeley, has been writer in residence at Smith College, and Zisskind Professor at Brandeis University.

Mr. Pritchett is married and lives in London.